"This resource is practical and [...] who are often forgotten with a painful loss. This is a much-needed book and will touch the lives of many."

—H. NORMAN WRIGHT, grief and trauma therapist, and author
of ninety books including *Recovering from the Loss of a Love*

"Mark Karris's *Season of Heartbreak* integrates the best of pastoral wisdom and clinical insights to craft a powerful and timely resource for those whose hearts ache after a painful breakup."

—ARCHIBALD D. HART, author of thirty-three books, and dean
emeritus and senior professor of psychology, Fuller Theological
Seminary

"Heartbreak. Loss. Grief. Healing. Mark Karris is simply masterful in *Season of Heartbreak*."

—TIM CLINTON, author of more than twenty books, licensed
counselor, and president of the American Association of Christian
Counselors

"A superb resource filled with real-life examples, deep insights, masterful metaphors, powerful practices, and contemporary research that will absolutely benefit you."

—SUSAN MEAD, author of *Dance with Jesus: From Grief to Grace*

"Integrating faith, clinical research, and helpful tools, Karris provides the compassion, hope, and grace that you need to mend your broken heart."

—KIM FREDRICKSON, licensed marriage and family therapist,
and author of *Give Yourself a Break*

"*Season of Heartbreak* is a much-needed travel companion for those of us seeking comfort and sanity after our heart has been broken in circumstances beyond our control. . . . Mark reminds us that a broken heart is meant to be tended to, that we were created to love and be loved, and that this wild, messy journey of human relationships is one of the greatest ways God leads us home."

—BETH ALLEN SLEVCOVE, spiritual director, and author
of *Broken Hallelujahs*

"Mark Karris has been through the painful terrain of heartbreak and helped many others through it. Beautifully weaving together biblical truths and contemporary science, *Season of Heartbreak* will help you make sense of your experience and guide you through hands-on practices for moving through heartbreak to hope and healing."

—TODD W. HALL, coauthor of *Psychology in the Spirit*, and professor of psychology and director of the Institute for Research on Psychology and Spirituality, Biola University

"Mark helps us learn to walk through grief so we can be, even in the pain, fully alive."

—JOSHUA STRAUB, cofounder and president of The Connextion Group, coauthor of *God Attachment*, and author of *Safe House*

"When loss comes to a heart, it is wise to seek counsel from trustworthy sources. Mark's prolific insights and suggestions offer wisdom and healing for the personal quest for relief and hope."

—CHRIS ANN WATERS, speaker, and author of *Seasons of Goodbye*

"In this book, Mark thoughtfully, purposefully, and vulnerably uses his unique perspective to help all of us take steps toward a deeper life of hope and freedom."

—SHAWN KENNEDY, pastor, and author of *Kingdom Come*

"I strongly recommend the passion, truth, and healing power of Jesus that flows through *Season of Heartbreak*. This book will expand the kingdom of God in your life."

—RONALD WALBORN, dean of Alliance Theological Seminary, and creator of the *Personal Spiritual Formation* DVD curriculum, 180 Media Group

"Experiencing loss is one of life's inevitable realities. . . . Mark Karris shows us a way forward that offers the kind of healing we all long for."

—RICH VILLODAS, lead pastor of New Life Fellowship Church

"*Season of Heartbreak* gently guides you through the darkness of grief and suffering while providing a step-by-step road map to health. With solid biblical underpinnings and supportive therapeutic research, Mark Karris's insights are well worth your investment. You'll come to know healing from the true Master of relationships: Jesus Christ."

—DONALD W. WELCH, president, founder, and CEO of Enriching Relationships, Inc.

"From his experience as a therapist and pastor, Mark Karris has written a marvelous book that offers hope for the brokenhearted. This is a must-read for anyone who has ever fallen in love only to have their heart broken."

—JAMES P. DANAHER, professor of philosophy, and author of *Contemplative Prayer* and *Jesus' Copernican Revolution*

"Mark Karris, with a wonderfully pastoral heart and keen clinical mind, has written a heartfelt book that encapsulates both sound theology and cutting-edge psychology in a rich and practical way. *Season of Heartbreak* is destined to help countless heartbroken Christians grieve well."

—KATHRYN DE BRUIN, CEO of Kathryn de Bruin Family Therapy and Training, and certified emotionally focused therapy trainer and supervisor

"With a compassionate tone and pastoral heart, Mark walks us through what can be expected in seasons of grief, and how to process these powerful emotions so that the outcome is a stronger heart and a more insightful life. Many Christians struggling with the derailing pain of loss will find this a helpful guide on their dark path."

—MARC ALAN SCHELSKE, pastor, and author of *The Spirituality of Emotions*

Season of Heartbreak

HEALING FOR THE HEART, BRAIN, AND SOUL

MARK GREGORY KARRIS

Kregel
Publications

To the downcast and brokenhearted,
and to those who refuse to allow "good-bye"
to be the last word in their sacred life story.

Contents

PART III: Grieving Practices

PART IV: Grieving Ponderings

Preface

There was a time when I was passionately and madly in love with someone. I thought I had met the woman of my dreams. I thought she was the one, God's lovingly providential pick for me. It felt heavenly. Every time I saw her I felt giddy and had a gleaming smile on my face. When we were apart, I couldn't wait until we saw each other again. Our love felt so real. Our relationship felt so right.

We cried together, laughed together, prayed together, and played together. We talked and whispered sweet nothings to each other on the phone every night, longing to see each other the next day. We even talked about marriage. We were both Christians who loved God, and we had similar hearts for ministry. Even though there were hardships in our relationship, I thought our love would get us through and we would be together forever. But I was wrong. Love didn't get us through. For various and complicated reasons, I got dumped.

I was devastated. I found myself lost in a sea of misery and despair. My heart felt as if it had been hit by a furious tornado. I didn't know how to cope. I was not sure how to deal with all the different emotions that overtook me. Even the encouragement and advice well-meaning friends and relatives offered were not helpful in easing the pain I felt deep inside. I looked for books and resources to help me through the painful process of breaking up with someone, but I couldn't find anything that spoke specifically to me as a heartbroken, emotional, wounded, and confused Christian.

Although growing through my suffering was not easy, I was determined to do it. So I decided to voraciously read everything I could on the subject of heartbreak and grief. I was interested in learning about my internal processes and emotional world. I wanted to find powerful practices to help me embrace grieving as a liberating spiritual discipline. I also found myself pondering deep theological questions about suffering and the will of God.

Years later, after grieving and healing from my own heartbreak, I married an amazing woman and became a licensed marriage and family therapist and ordained pastor. Since then I have worked with countless grieving and heartbroken people. Drawing on their experiences and my own, I have written the book I wish had been available to me when I needed it. I pray its contents will prove an invaluable resource to help you grieve well and heal your broken heart.

Acknowledgments

I am truly grateful for the support, patience, grace, and love I have experienced from my incredible wife, Bianca. You have loved me into life.

I am thankful for countless friends, colleagues, and mentors for their helpful feedback, support, and encouragement. I would also like to thank the incredible folks at Kregel Publications and my fantastic editor Sarah De Mey. It takes a village.

I am deeply touched by many of the courageous clients, friends, and fellow travelers who have shared their painful, yet triumphant, stories with me.

I am also in awe of, and thankful for, God's kindness and redeeming love.

Introduction

Do you remember whispering sweet nothings to the person you thought was going to be your soul mate? Do you remember holding hands with that person, feeling as if the divine bliss would never end? Did you take long walks and let magical breezes gently caress your faces on quiet spring mornings? Did you tell yourself the two of you were meant to be together—that this was the one you were destined to spend the rest of your life with? Sure there were occasions of fighting, disagreeing, and bickering, but that didn't matter because God had brought the two of you together and you were deeply in love, right? And because your hearts were surrendered to God and intertwined with one another, you thought your relationship would last forever, right?

Unfortunately, many of us eventually find out that is not always the case. In fact, love can suck! No, it really can. It can suck the life right out of us, especially when it leaves us with torn, battered, and shattered hearts in its aftermath.

Miraculously, there are people in the world who have never had their hearts broken by betrayal, affairs, unforeseen personality clashes, and irreconcilable differences (but I can count their number on one hand). There really are people who fall in love, give their hearts to someone, and sail off into the sunset while singing praise songs to God. I think that is wonderful.

Season of Heartbreak, however, is not intended for those who have happily sailed into the sunset. It is for those whose sails have been tragically torn and who are unable to mend them. It is for those who gave their all for love and now feel as though the sun will never rise again. It is for those who can't boast about a one-hit-wonder lover. This book is for those who have been left in agony to pick up the remnants of a tender heart. *Season of Heartbreak* is for the heartbroken who doubt themselves, who doubt God, and who wonder if they will ever love or be loved again.

This book is meant to fill the gaps that well-meaning friends, family, and church communities try to fill with their advice and support. No one is to blame when the advice turns out to be ill fitted, but good advice is crucial and those who care about us are not always equipped to deal with our world-shattering loss. Those spending time with us every day tend to underestimate the complex web of disillusionment and grief we suffer. Fact is, shallow responses can simply add to our pain—dare I say "trauma" for some? "There are plenty of other fish in the sea." "Cheer up. God has someone better for you." "Be encouraged. God will work it out for the good." While these responses may all be true, they offer little consolation to heartbroken people.

Season of Heartbreak: Healing for the Heart, Brain, and Soul is a practical guide to healing and transformation for those whose hearts are broken after the loss of love. *Season of Heartbreak* combines spiritual, theological, and psychological research with practical real-world experiences. It is designed to help heartbroken people navigate through the unknown—and sometimes disorienting—territory of grief, heal from pain, and ultimately let God use their experiences to transform their lives. Although this book can be a powerful resource for all types of grievers, it is primarily for those whose hearts are broken because a dating or marital relationship has ended. It is also a helpful tool for counselors, pastors, and family members who want a refresher course on heartbreak, grief, and helping hurting loved ones.

Season of Heartbreak: Healing for the Heart, Brain, and Soul is written with the assumption that emotional and spiritual health are deeply connected—integral—to life's journey. Peter Scazzero, who wrote *The Emotionally Healthy Church,* says, "Emotional health and spiritual health are inseparable—[and] will amount to a Copernican revolution for many in the Christian community. It is not possible for a Christian to be spiritually mature while remaining emotionally immature."[1] And part of the aim of this book is to help you gain emotional and spiritual insights, skills, and practices that will help you grieve well now and remain to serve you throughout your life's journey.

This book is divided into four parts. The content of the first part, "Grieving Processes," is just what it sounds like—the process and nuances of grief. It begins with defining terms such as *grief* and *loss* and then discusses common experiences as a way to help you normalize and understand your own oftentimes chaotic grieving process. This section also examines the patterns of grief, the nature of hurt, the power of emotions, and the avoidance of pain (shock absorbers), and it ends with the final transition—letting go.

The second part, "Grieving Pathways," discusses vital relational pathways with God, others, and self as you grieve the loss of love. It also looks at obstacles and debris that can block those pathways and keep you from having future life-giving connections.

The third part, "Grieving Practices," discusses real-world spiritual practices you can engage in to help you heal, grieve, and take ownership of your journey through heartbreak. We will explore diverse practices such as grieving, journaling, weeping, self-compassion, traveling with others along their pathways, forgiving, and other practices to help you successfully progress toward healing.

The last part, "Grieving Ponderings," comprises cultural and theological reflections that inform, educate, and inspire new ways of looking at the sacred art of listening.

Are you grieving a broken heart at this very moment? If so, will you let me—someone who has crossed the minefield of heartbreak, someone equipped to guide you safely to the other side—reach back and offer you my hand? My sole purpose in writing this book is to provide a powerful, life-giving resource that will help you not only survive your season of grief but also thrive and be transformed. Please know that you are not alone.

PART I

Grieving Processes

This section is designed to help you understand the nature of grief and the emotional process you are going through in your difficult season of heartbreak. The aftermath of heartbreak and grief can oftentimes leave you feeling confused and frightened because you are not only moving into uncharted territory, but even worse, you feel as though you are the only one inhabiting this strange new land. With a greater understanding of the nature of grief and your emotional process, however, you will be able to reduce your suffering, diminish your feeling of aloneness, and achieve a greater ability to grieve well and heal.

CHAPTER 1

Zigzag

Even in laughter the heart may ache,
and rejoicing may end in grief.
—PROVERBS 14:13

When Montu opened in 1996 at Busch Gardens in Florida, it was the tallest and fastest roller coaster in the world. There are moments on that ride in which you are completely inverted, and you will experience 3.8 times the force of gravity.[1] At the time of Montu's unveiling, there was also a Nile crocodile exhibit below part of the track, making the ride both stunning to look at and terrifying as you plummeted toward the crocodile pit. It was truly a sight to behold and a treacherously amazing experience. Oh, and did I mention that Montu was the name of an ancient god who was known as the god of war?

It is quite common for those who are grieving a breakup to feel as if they are on an unpredictable, out-of-control, zigzagging roller coaster. While at some points along the way, people feel a profound heaviness as though pinned down by g-force, looking at the hungry crocodiles wanting to eat away at a hopeful future, at other points, they feel steady, secure, and optimistic about the journey ahead, as though rolling across a straight, smooth path.

You have experienced a profound *loss*, a literal breaking or tearing apart of the most powerful and intimate bond a person can have. As a result of that loss, you are experiencing overwhelming grief, which entails a kaleidoscope of feelings. The deeper you have loved, the greater the loss and the more profound the grief. The grieving process you are now going through is the natural means of fully experiencing the feelings that accompany the loss so you can heal from your heartbreak, learn valuable life lessons, and with pen in hand, write the next chapter of your ever unfolding life adventure.

Even though the grieving process is normal and necessary after experiencing heartbreak, the path is not linear. Unfortunately, there is no God-ordained *Seven Steps to Freedom: An Approach to Grief After Getting Dumped* manual you can buy online or ask God to throw down with a parachute from his heavenly archives. People are way too complex and their stories and experiences are too drastically different to fit into that pre-packaged, neatly designed, one-size-fits-all approach. In reality, grieving is more like a zigzag; a lightning bolt; an up-and-down slanted, messy trail, as unique as the individual going through it.

Examples of Zigzags

Some people get their hearts broken and shrug it off. In the beginning, they tell themselves, "I don't care. The other person is the one who is missing out. It's their loss." But within a few days, they find themselves calling their exes, begging them to come back. When their exes push them away again, they resort to a nonchalant attitude, pretending their exes could only dream of being with them. That back-and-forth dance can happen a dozen times until those who got dumped finally come to a place of acceptance (or denial) and find someone else to replace their ex.

Others have a more chaotic and confusing zigzag. One minute they are bawling, curled up in the fetal position and feeling as if their world has come crashing down. The next minute, they are furious. The next minute they are okay, cracking a smile at a joke a friend is telling them. Then back to the fetal position (that was probably me!). This cycle can go on for months. Then a year passes, and just when they think they are more stable and finally getting over their exes, they hear a love song that sends them into a spiral of grief, which could take a few hours or even days to get out of. Eventually, however, the storm clouds pass, the sun comes out in full radiance, and they are ready for the next hello.

We don't get our heart broken and then transition smoothly through meticulously mapped-out stages and phases of grief. That would be amazing if it were the case, though. That predictability would make the process so much more manageable.

Keep in mind that this is *your* messy zigzag, and it will look different from what everybody else has experienced. Don't let anyone force his or her zigzag on you. Don't listen to the naysayers of grief or those who have an aversion to all things messy and emotional. Don't let people guilt you into moving on. Pay no attention to those who say, "Thus saith the Lord, 'You have grieved long enough, so move on already.'" While listening to feedback from those closest to you is important, ultimately this is your journey, with your unique timetable for grieving. You have a divinely designed, tailor-made path to healing. Only you can determine when you have walked fully through the twists and turns of the valley of the shadow of grief.

Consequences of Avoidance

You must embark on a journey to intentionally grieve your breakup, and it will take every ounce of courage you can muster. Some decide that being intentional about grieving well is too much for them and instead take shortcuts to numb the pain.

They believe that if they go about their normal routines, then time will heal all wounds. If you decide to fight, avoid, or suppress the loss and pain of your heartbreak, you will actually make it worse.

Among the most common symptoms of grieving are what we call intrusive thoughts, which are usually unwelcome and unpleasant thoughts about you and your ex—thoughts about what happened in the past, thoughts about what you should or shouldn't have done, and anxious thoughts about the future. Research shows that the more you try to push away your thoughts and wish you were thinking about something else, the more you will have the thoughts you didn't want in the first place.[2] The effect is similar to me saying to you, "Don't think of a smiling elephant with polka dots. I mean it. Don't think of a smiling elephant with polka dots." And then, guess what? You are thinking about a smiling elephant with polka dots.

Pushing away and avoiding the grieving process will invariably not serve you well in the long run. The only way to grieve well and heal from heartbreak is to come to a place of radical acceptance, however difficult the road may be.

Acceptance

Jesus suffered a heartbreak of biblical proportions. Unlike those of us who were blindsided by our breakup, Jesus was clued in to what was going to happen. His loving and deeply connected relationship with God the Father was going to be severed for a time. In Mark 14:33–36 we see that Jesus knew he was about to feel the horror of abandonment by the One he loved. He was "deeply distressed and troubled." Days before the devastating event, Jesus told his friends, "My soul is overwhelmed with sorrow to the point of death." Although Jesus prayed to avoid the impending torture, ridicule, betrayal, abandonment, and grief ("take this cup from me"), he ultimately accepted his fate and prayed, "Yet not what I will, but what you will."

Like Jesus, you might experience moments in which you wish things were different. That is understandable. Acceptance doesn't mean you have to like your circumstances or not wish for a different outcome. Acceptance is an inner openness to the way it really is in the present moment. I encourage you to model your response after Jesus's resilient attitude; embrace what is currently set before you, trusting that God's ultimate plan and purpose for your life will unfold.

The truth is that there is no switch you can flip or special prayer you can pray to be instantly done with the grieving process. While there are healthy practices for grieving well, there is no surefire way to pull the zigzag's ends and make a straight line of predictability and instant healing. The best thing you can do is not fight for a different outcome and come to a place where you can accept yourself, your season of grief, and your road to healing.

As you embark on this journey to understand the nuances of your unique zigzag and overall process of grief, it is my hope that you can cultivate the attitude of acceptance. You are stuck in the grieving process, so you might as well be open to it and see what you can learn from it while having a compassionate attitude toward yourself. Punching your zigzag in the face to try to knock it down or get away from it will not do you any good. Seeking to understand and accept your zigzag without denying it, as you allow God to hold your hand and gently guide you through the healing process, will produce far better results.

Like the phoenix rising from the ashes, you will rise from this tempestuous trial with a fiery love, fierce compassion, and discerning wisdom you have never known before if you accept the healing journey before you and surrender the process to God. I know, it's easier said than done. You might think that healing and growth are located in a galaxy far, far away. My prayer is that God will grant you the serenity to accept the things you cannot change, the courage to change the things you can, the wisdom to know the difference, and the patience to wait for God's incredible transformation to unfold both in and through your life.[3]

Now that we have used a broad brush to paint a general picture of your grief process, let's look at some of the details and common dynamics of people who experience heartbreak.

CHAPTER 2

Ouch! That Hurts!

You will hurt. Pain is the natural result of loss,
especially when a dream dies. When there's a hole
in your life, pain fills it for a time. This is normal.
—NORMAN WRIGHT, *Recovering from the Loss of a Love*

When the person you love tells you that he or she does not want to be with you anymore, your world shatters; time stands still; your heart beats a million miles an hour, and you feel as though it will jump out of your chest and run down the street without you. Your thoughts race out of control; they are so fast you can't hear any of them. You feel as if you are breathing through a straw. The apocalypse of the soul has come. Your world as you knew it is devastatingly over.

We hear every day that someone has divorced their spouse or separated from their love interest; nevertheless, you were unprepared for the trauma when your own breakup and loss occurred. As with most people, the reality of your own breakup is too hard to bear. When it happens, your internalized and fortified myth that "love will last forever" comes crashing down, and you are jolted, shell-shocked, and incapacitated. Next to the death of someone you love, the end of a romantic relationship may be the single most painful and heart-wrenching experience you can go through. It hurts. It really, really hurts.

Hurt and Tylenol

Speaking of hurt, what is it? Hurt is a cocktail of feelings such as anger, sadness, and fear that you can literally feel pulsating through your whole body. Have you ever noticed that people use the word *hurt* to describe both physical and emotional pain? That is because people feel both types of pain in the same region of the brain.[1] As far as the brain is concerned, the emotional pain you feel after breaking up with the person you love most equals the physical pain of getting hit from behind with a huge brick.

Have you ever taken acetaminophen? I bet you have. Another name for it is Tylenol. In a recent study, researchers hypothesized that, if people feel physical pain and emotional pain in the same regions of the brain, then acetaminophen could possibly help reduce emotional pain.

Researchers administered acetaminophen to some of the participants and a placebo (a fake pill) to the others for three weeks straight. The researchers then hurt the participants' feelings by excluding them from an activity, causing them to feel rejection, and then hooked them up to a functional magnetic resonance imaging (fMRI) machine, which examines the brain. The researchers concluded that those who received the acetaminophen reported hurt feelings less frequently than did the placebo group, which demonstrates significant overlap between emotional and physical pain as registered by the brain.[2]

People can see a badly bruised arm and understand how painful it is because they can view it with their own eyes. If only people could see the bruise on your heart and know how much it hurts. Experiencing a breakup cuts to the deepest core of your emotional, physical, and spiritual being. Emotional pain is real.

Feels Like a Death

A recent study proved that the grief suffered by someone who has experienced a breakup is similar to the grief suffered by someone who has experienced the death of a loved one.[3] Researchers gathered participants who had experienced a breakup and told them to look at pictures of their exes and remember the times they shared with them. The participants were connected to an fMRI machine to identify the areas of the brain affected as the participants looked at their exes' photos. The study revealed the following:

> The areas of the brain affected by a breakup are the same areas affected by cocaine use (the anterior nucleus accumbens, for you brain nerds). I will discuss more on this point later.

> The areas of the brain affected by a breakup are the same areas affected by mourning the death of a loved one.

Though the emotional pain of rejection and the emotional pain caused by the death of a loved one clearly occur because of two very different events, your brain and nervous system register them as the same thing. There are differences, however, between grieving a heartbreak and grieving someone's passing.

For example, while a person can feel abandoned by someone who has passed away, the experience is much different than the rejection and blow to one's self-esteem experienced in a breakup. The loss of a romantic partner causes you to question your core belief in yourself, and your self-esteem may be reduced to the size of a pinhead. You may start wondering whether you are tainted goods and whether you will ever be lovable enough to attract someone else again.

Another difference between the two is that when someone dies, you have no chance of getting that person back. A natural but difficult grieving process can take place when someone dies, and after a period of time, you can accept the fact that your loved one is gone. But when you are in a relationship and the other person suddenly breaks up with you, or you have to break up with them, he or she does not go away. Your ex still lives on this planet. You might even work with that person, have the same friends on Facebook, attend the same church, or live in the same town. Any of these scenarios can make your breakup all the more complicated.

Though both losses hurt deeply, they hurt deeply in different ways.

Ugh . . . Your Ex Is Still Around

It is important to detail the unique types of hurt and emotional pain that occur when your ex is still around. When you and your significant other break up, one of two painful scenarios occurs. The first scenario has that person's very presence on the planet annoying the heaven out of you. He or she is still able to contact you, play mind games, say something stupid on some social media site, or do something else that irritates you. This behavior usually occurs when the breakup resulted from the other person being incompatible, crazy, a jerk, or all three. You loved him or her, and even though you really didn't want to break up, for any number of reasons, you had to do it.

Let's examine a common relationship scenario with Sarah and Shawn. They met through mutual friends and were instantly attracted to each other. Shawn seemed so nice and genuine. He opened the car door for Sarah, listened intently to her stories, and bought her gifts. They enjoyed spending a lot of time together. They loved hiking together, going to the movies, and dining at nice restaurants. Sarah gave her heart to him rather quickly. She was madly in love.

About six months into the relationship, Shawn suddenly began to change. He became increasingly distant and erratic, and he very easily lost patience with Sarah. She suspected he was either seeing someone else or doing drugs. She was not sure what was going on with him. She tried to talk with him about her concerns, but he quickly changed the subject. Even though she loved him, she knew if he kept being a jerk, she would have to leave.

After a few incidents that she considered abusive, Sarah was done with the relationship. Despite feeling torn, she knew she had to break up with Shawn. It proved to be one of the hardest things she'd ever done. Shawn took it badly and became even more of a jerk. He started calling and texting her incessantly. He wrote inappropriate things about her on their mutual friends' Facebook walls. Because they had the same circle of friends, she occasionally saw him at parties or gatherings, and he always made a scene.

Sarah was frustrated in her goal of grieving the loss of the relationship they once had, because Shawn's close proximity often produced emotional triggers. Sarah wanted to move on and grieve well, but Shawn's looming presence constantly put a wrench in the works.

The second painful dynamic that can happen when the ex is still around is actually the opposite of the first. Instead of wanting to move on and grieve well, you can become obsessed with trying to get back together with the other person. Since your ex is not dead, you may very well irrationally believe you can rekindle the fiery passion the two of you once shared. You can make yourself believe all kinds of things to convince yourself the relationship could work out after all. For example, you may say to yourself,

"I can't live without my boyfriend, and he can't live without me. He just needs time to see that."

"How could she throw away all the special feelings and times we shared? I know she still loves me and will come back to me."

"If I stop sinning and pray hard enough, God will give me the desires of my heart and bring my boyfriend back to me."

Letting go is hard for a person caught in this dynamic. Such a person is desperate to escape the painful heartache and get back to feeling whole again with the person he or she still loves.

Addicted to Love

Another reason breaking up with someone is so painful is that we miss how our special lover made us feel. Being in love produces a hotbed of neurochemicals such as the neurotransmitters of oxytocin (otherwise known as the "cuddle hormone") and dopamine (otherwise known as the "feel-good neurotransmitter"). Every time we see, hear, or touch our romantic partner, we are awash in these drugs.

Research proves it. Remember the photograph study? When the participants looked at pictures of their exes, the brain's reward centers lit up on the fMRI monitor the same way they would during cocaine use. Simply looking at a picture and thinking about an ex-partner is like being injected with an addictive drug. Imagine the quantity of neurochemicals triggered when they are actually with their partners face-to-face.

Those who lose love can be like addicts without their fix, desperately searching for their exes' embrace to soothe their anxious souls and dopamine-deprived bodies. They miss the high of the special love and connection they once knew. They are thirsty for that which only the cocktail of their lover's embrace and affirmation can supply. They are "faint with love" (Song 5:8).

I know it sounds weird, and I don't want to reduce a sacred,

God-given gift to mere chemical reactions, but these neuro-chemicals play a key role in creating love, as well as the viscerally painful experience of the loss of love. The reality is that the excruciating pain and anguish felt in the loss of love is similar to that felt in the withdrawal stage of an addiction. When the reality of a breakup sets in, a person can experience all types of debilitating emotions and feelings, similar to how drug addicts feel when they can't get their fix. Some will beg, manipulate, bargain, and do many irrational things to get their significant other back, much like a drug addict who will do anything to feel that high again.

Now please hear me. I am not saying this to pathologize anyone. I am not calling anyone an addict in a demeaning way. I am only saying that God designed us in such a way that we become emotionally, spiritually, and physically tethered to those we give our hearts, souls, or bodies to—in biblical terms, those with whom we become "one flesh" (Gen. 2:24). Powerful neuro-chemicals are part of what not only draws two people together in the first place but also helps them stay together and remain faithful to one another throughout their lives. When we undo or tear apart the one-flesh connection, we experience normal but very painful mind, body, and spirit consequences.

It Is Supposed to Hurt

You are not possessed by a legion of demons. You do not have "a vile spirit of heartache" that needs to be cast out. If you went hiking, tripped over a rock, fell into a stream, and broke your leg, that break would hurt like heck. That is normal. Experiencing heartache when a person you genuinely loved and felt safe with leaves is also normal. Heartbreak is agony. It is painful. It hurts. And thank God it does not have to remain that way. As a broken leg needs to be properly set and put in a cast if it is to heal well, so your broken heart needs to be properly tended. There are certain pathways, practices, and mind-sets you can engage in that will help you heal. We will consider those in parts II and III of this book.

CHAPTER 3

Powerful Emotions

Grief surprised me; it has been nothing like I expected. I felt anger one hour and acceptance the next; then it was back to anger and on to regret with a bit of exhaustion and joy, gratitude, and astonishment thrown in for good measure.
—REBEKAH L. MILES, *When the One You Love Is Gone*

Powerful emotions are fueling your unique grief process, similar to the way electricity is propelling Montu in Florida. In Latin, the word *emotion* means "to move." Emotions are moving you in all sorts of directions as the reality of a breakup starts to settle in and unsettle you.

Emotions are some of the most electric and compelling forces on the planet. Grief, for example, can be so great that you have trouble concentrating at work or school. Anxiety can be so great that it causes insomnia—affecting your ability to fall or stay asleep—or it can affect your ability to eat. Despair can trigger negative thoughts, such as "I am worthless" and "No one will ever love me again." Due to sadness, one minute you are crying, the next minute you think you are okay, and suddenly you are sobbing again.

Maybe you have not cried at all. Perhaps the only emotion

you feel is anger, and you find yourself in a bad mood all the time. You're angry at your boss. You're angry at your dog. You're angry at yourself and the world. Perhaps you are confused because you don't know what the heck is wrong with you. You know you do not feel okay. Emotions are powerful and can affect you in all kinds of ways.

Experiencing the jolt of emotions is normal. You loved deeply, giving your heart; you might have thought you would spend the rest of your life together. You are grieving a profound loss of connection, attachment, intimacy, conversation, affectionate touch, hopes, and dreams. You have every right to grieve and feel the way you do. I encourage you to feel, and to feel deeply and wholly, even though we live in a culture that doesn't always allow you to (more about that in part IV).

Name to Tame

One of the hardest dynamics of the grieving process to endure is the confusion that sets in because of your chaotic emotional experience. Your inability to understand what is going on creates more anxiety and additional suffering. Once you are able to understand your emotional experience and have emotional intelligence (EQ), you are able to tranquilize your amygdala, which is one of the main areas of your brain triggering your emotional roller coaster. Research shows that when you can name your emotion and understand your experience, you can tame it and experience a greater sense of calm.[1] Matthew Lieberman, an esteemed researcher on this topic, wrote in the *New York Times*, "If the amygdala is like an alarm clock alerting us to potential threats, putting feelings into words is like hitting the snooze button."[2]

Four months after breaking up with her boyfriend, Victoria

came to see me. She thought she needed to see a therapist because she was crying all the time, lacked motivation, and felt anxious when she went to church. She told me she was a leader in her church and that many people looked up to her as a strong woman of God. When she was with her staff and members of the congregation, she tried hard not to let people see the grief she was experiencing. I could tell, however, that she was in tremendous pain.

"I don't know what is wrong with me," she said as tears started rolling down her cheeks. "I am supposed to be strong, and God is supposed to be my everything. Why am I feeling this way? Is there something wrong with me?"

I started to enter into her painful experience and deeply empathize with her. "I can see you are in tremendous pain right now," I said. "This is really hard. Can we stay here with these feelings a minute?"

After allowing her to experience her full range of emotions and reveal her story, I wanted to normalize her struggle. I briefly shared how I went through a heartbreak in the past and could attest to its devastation, even as a Christian leader. I helped her understand how, one by one, each emotion she felt had something valuable to tell her. As the session went on, I watched her take deep breaths and begin to calm down.

At the end of the session, she said, "Thank you. All these months I thought I was going crazy. What you said makes total sense. I thought that something was wrong with me and that God didn't love me. But you have helped me understand these crazy emotions I have been having. I am still hurting, but I do feel lighter and can breathe a little bit easier."

Many times the chaos and confusion of our emotional experiences make them seem overwhelming. But when we can understand and even befriend our experiences through the compassionate gaze of a trusted person, they become more bearable.

What Are Emotions?

Let's examine the purpose of emotions, not only so we can better understand what we are going through in our season of heartbreak, but also so we feel less as if we're riding on the Montu roller coaster and more as if we're riding on the Bugs Bunny Barnstormer, an easygoing kids' ride at the famous theme park Great Adventure. We can still have lows and highs, but they will be much more manageable.

Emotions are part of a God-given GPS (if you will) that allows us to know where we are, where we want to go, and how to get there.[3] All emotions convey powerful information and have their own unique built-in plea for action. Emotions may not always convey accurate information about objective truth, but they always point to valuable subjective truth within the individual. Emotions do not have to lead to ultimate conclusions or definitively determine a person's course of action, but when listened to prayerfully, they can help navigate this beautifully chaotic and wondrous world with greater skill and awareness.

You might be surprised to learn that your emotions are God-given and helpful. I was. Initially I was wary of emotions and considered propositions, thinking, and reasoning to be the primary vehicles to truth and to living the Christian life. I thought emotions were inferior, untruthful, unspiritual, and fleshly. My early church experiences were filled with people who thought emotions were troublesome demons that needed to be quickly cast out of hurting people.

I will never forget this man I knew who was in the throes of grief. He was unbearably distressed because his girlfriend broke up with him. He was a wreck, so he decided to go to church for solace and community. The people at church could see he was a mess, so after the service they quickly gathered around him like bees and began to sting him with passionate and bold prayers, such as "I bind the spirit of sadness in the name of Jesus" and "You come out of him, you spirit of depression and anger." They thought that by ridding him of those nasty varmints (emotions), he would be restored and free again.

That approach is at best unfounded and at worst harmful. Don't get me wrong; praying for others is a sacred and beautiful experience, but it is absurd to call naturally occurring, God-given emotions demons or to try to cast them out.

I don't believe emotions are bad, sinful, or demonic. However, there are times when the effects of sin can cause our emotions—our GPS—to go haywire. Some healthy emotions can morph into unhealthy ones. What was meant to trigger healthy guilt, for example, can morph quickly into unhealthy shame. Anger can serve as a cover-up or defense against feeling the more tender emotion of sadness. For some people, fear can rise up when they experience love and kindness from someone who cares deeply about them. Being unable to decipher what is going on with our emotional experiences, or manage them appropriately, leaves us vulnerable to being confused, crushed, or carelessly controlled by them.

In reality, some of the most common problems surrounding emotions are not the emotions themselves but the defenses and strategies we use to deal or not deal with them. For example, some people call a friend, pray to God, or read a good book when they feel sad and lonely, but others watch pornography or go on ill-advised shopping sprees. Some people petition for passage of better laws when they get angry, but others get into fistfights. Feeling strong emotions is not the problem, but what you do as a result may be (more about that in the next chapter).

The Wisdom of Emotions

Because sin can affect our emotional GPS, we should allow the Holy Spirit to help us use rational thinking that aligns with the principles of love and God's Word to process our emotions. This is what the phrase "the mind of Christ" is referring to in 1 Corinthians 2:16.[4]

In the rest of this chapter I want to give you a peek into the power and wisdom of the most common emotions experienced during heartbreak. Our ability to understand emotional experiences is vital to our grieving well.

The following chart details the wisdom of emotions. Note the emotions you have experienced lately.

	Communicates Information	Built-in Plea for Action
Sadness	Tells us there has been a loss	Moves us to seek solace, nurturing, and care from others
Fear	Tells us there is danger	Moves us to fight, flee, or freeze
Disgust	Tells us something is toxic or foul	Moves us to turn away from and avoid
Joy	Tells us a goal has been reached	Moves us to open up, stay engaged, or share with others
Anger	Tells us a goal has been frustrated or something is unjust or unfair	Moves us to right the wrong and make a change
Guilt	Tells us our behaviors or thoughts are contrary to our values or those of our community	Moves us to reconcile, make amends, and restore relationship
Unhealthy Shame	Tells us *we* are wrong for our behaviors or thoughts, which are contrary to our values or those of our community	Moves us to hide, attack ourselves or others, or engage in run-and-numb activities such as defenses or addictions

Now let's examine anger, sadness, and shame in more detail to see how they can move us in unique ways through the grieving process after a breakup.

In the initial stages of a breakup, many people feel a lot of *anger* because they think they were betrayed. When people suffer breakups, they are often deeply shocked. They can't believe their partner is no longer in love with them and is now leaving. They feel angry because they think life is totally unfair and believe their partner has treated them unjustly. Not all people feel this angry, especially if they had to break up for sensible reasons or if the breakup was amicable. Many people do get angry, however, and the proverb is true, "An angry person stirs up conflict, and a hot-tempered person commits many sins" (Prov. 29:22). Unfortunately, not everyone knows how to manage the emotion of anger and will try to "right a wrong" in the wrong kind of way, ultimately causing more pain. There is a way to listen to what the emotion of anger is telling you without committing "many sins."

Jason, a young man I was counseling, was livid that his girlfriend broke up with him over the phone. He told me he felt betrayed. (As an aside, a person cannot "feel betrayed." Being broken up with is the stimulus or the act considered betrayal. Anger is the emotion that a person might feel because of the act of betrayal.) Jason called her repeatedly and harassed her over the phone. He even stooped so low as to stalk her at her job. He couldn't let the relationship go. Jason allowed his anger to move him to do things that ultimately caused him more pain. Out the window went the verse that says, "In your anger do not sin" (Eph. 4:26). Letting anger get the best of him kept him from God, a loving community, self-reflection, and learning powerful lessons he could have used in his next relationship. His inability to respond appropriately to his anger kept him from grieving well.

Linda was another person I met with. She and her boyfriend found each other online. Slowly, she began giving him her heart and trusting him. After eleven months together, she found out he was cheating on her. She became profoundly angry because of his unjust betrayal. Linda listened to her anger and used it appropriately. Instead of directing her anger solely at her ex, she directed the angry energy toward making a positive decision for her ultimate good; she assertively broke off the relationship, reached out to family and friends for comfort, and healthily grieved the loss of relationship with her boyfriend.

Sadness is another common emotion experienced during heartbreak. Sadness penetrates deep to the core of who you are and communicates to you there has been a loss. In this case the loss is your sweetheart, your lover, the person who might know more about you than anybody else in the world. Experiencing sadness is a sign that your heart is alive and not dead, calloused, or cold. It is a proof that you loved deeply. Sadness, along with its built-in plea for action, wants to move you toward a comforting and caring connection with God and others during this difficult time.

Interestingly enough, the soft and warm emotion of sadness is usually behind the hard and hot emotion of anger. Every person immersed in anger and blaming and cursing the ex is a guy or girl who is deeply hurt and sad. Many times anger is just covering up and deflecting the sadness. Only when you can sit and process the hurt, sadness, and pain can you move on from the anger.

DeAndre met Abby at a friend's party. They hit it off instantly and connected on so many levels. They loved the same movies, served at the downtown homeless shelter, and attended the same church. After a few years, however, Abby fell out of love with DeAndre. She no longer had the feelings for him she once had. Even though she didn't quite understand how she currently felt about them as a couple, she tried to explain her "falling out of love" with him as best she could, and that she knew she had to move on.

At first, DeAndre was angry, because, in his mind, Abby hadn't provided an adequate reason for breaking up with him. After trying many times to understand her perspective, however, he finally gave up. (He later learned that she had, in fact, met someone else.) Even though DeAndre was angry, he knew there was a lot of sadness behind his anger, because he was able to control his emotions while allowing himself to experience them.

He refused to let the anger swell up and move him to dishonor himself or the woman he loved. He may not have completely understood her decision at the time, but he respected it nonetheless. He knew his sadness was telling him about the great loss he was experiencing, and he knew the best thing he could do was listen to the sadness, pour his heart out to God, reach out to a few friends on a weekly basis, and seek a therapist's help to work out the grief on a deeper level. Emotions are wise teachers if we can listen to them.

The last emotion I want to talk about, as it relates to heartbreak, is *shame*. Brené Brown, a well-known scholar on shame, says, "We all experience shame. We're all afraid to talk about it. And, the less we talk about it, the more we have it."[5] Those who have had a breakup or a divorce are more susceptible to this silent, joy-stealing emotion.

Guilt is an emotion experienced after one has *done* something wrong, whereas shame is an experience that communicates to an individual that he or she *is* something wrong. Shame, especially after a breakup, can send the message to us that we are unlovable, tainted, dirty, flawed, and no good. Shame causes us to weigh twenty-five, fifty, or seventy-five pounds more than we actually weigh in our spirits. Lewis Smedes writes that shame is "a vague, undefined heaviness that presses on our spirit, dampens our gratitude for the goodness of life, and slackens the free flow of joy. Shame . . . seeps into and discolors all our other feelings, primarily about ourselves, but about almost everyone and everything else in our life as well."[6]

On many occasions shame is guilt gone rogue and has nothing to do with the oxygen of heaven. When referring to the inner emotional experience we have when we miss the mark (sin) regarding our actions, nonactions, and thoughts, I prefer the term *healthy guilt* or the biblical phrase *godly sorrow*. Worldly sorrow (unhealthy shame) leads to death, but godly sorrow leads to life with no yucky residue (2 Cor. 7:10). Godly sorrow is an inner remorse one feels because of sinful behavior or inaction and has a built-in plea for action, which prioritizes relationships and moves a person to right their wrongs.

Shame is a debilitating emotion that has no rightful place in the heart of a child of God. Shame is one of the most harmful emotions that exist within the human experience, especially when it festers and darkens one's view of oneself, God, and others. It contributes to much of our suffering and catapults us into addictions, self-harm, and harming others. I know those are bold statements, but there is plenty of research to back them up.[7]

I know from my own experience and from the experiences of those I have counseled that shame can skyrocket after a breakup. After being rejected, the heartbroken person commonly feels unwanted and becomes self-critical. Here are some shame statements that people have shared with me after their breakups:

"I feel like trash. I deserve to be alone."

"I feel horrible about myself. Who in their right mind is going to want me at this age? I might as well join a convent."

"I feel God doesn't like me, like I did something wrong for this to happen. Truth is, there were a lot of sinful things I did in the relationship. I think God is punishing me."

"I must not be pretty enough for him. If I am, then why did he leave me for that bimbo? This sucks! I just feel so ugly all the time."

"I feel so much shame. I am a leader in my church. I should have it more together. I fail in every relationship I am in. I feel like a big loser."

"You want to know why I watch porn? It's because it helps me feel good for a little bit during my boring, vain existence. Obviously, I am not good enough for a girl to like me, or else she would have stayed with me. Porn helps me cope."

I remember experiencing a lot of shame after my breakup years ago. Truth be told, I felt a lot of shame *before* my breakup. There was always a low-level hum of toxic shame creeping its way into many thoughts I had about myself and about the way other people saw me. The breakup just magnified my core ideas that I was unlovable and worthless, and that no one would ever love me again.

At first, shame moved me to isolate myself and attack myself with my thoughts. After all, if I believed I was unlovable, then why would I think anyone else would want to be around me? Once shame gained that foothold in my mind, I jumped into another relationship on the rebound just to feel lovable again. (By the way, I don't recommend this. Rebound relationships rarely ever pan out.) All the while, shame kept me from entering the presence of God in prayer. I thought God was angry with me and no longer liked me—since he callously caused my heartbreak and ruined my life—so why would I want to spend time with him?

Shame is a stealthy thief! It subtly robs us of life's goodness and beauty and keeps us from the crucial relationships that matter most to us. If you have recently broken up with someone, please know the experience of shame is more common than you think. You are not alone, and there is hope. I have encountered hope firsthand, and his name is Jesus.

Jesus touched and embraced the losers, lepers, liars, lunatics, loose lovers, loose livers, outcasts, and every other marginalized misfit, and he healed them and freed them from the grip of shame. Even when they ashamedly cried out:

"No, you don't know who I am!"

"You don't know what I've done!"

"You don't know which disease I have!"

"You won't be able to stand the smell!"

"You don't know how many husbands I've had!"

"You don't know how much I've stolen!"

Jesus said to them, in effect, "Yes, I do know who you are! I no longer remember what you've done! And there is no sin or stench that can keep me away from you!" And then he proceeded to touch them, hold them, and heal them.

God sent Jesus not only to live and die for you but also to love away your shame and give you a new identity. He wants you to know that even with your imperfections, failures, and frailty, you are a new creation. You are his beloved, bestowed with honor and dignity. You are not worthless, but priceless.

Emotions Are Messy but Vital

The Giver (2014), a movie based on a book of the same name, focuses on a community that had made a decision to eradicate suffering and maintain peace at any cost. To accomplish this, the authoritative elders of the community forced people to take medication that removed their ability to feel deep emotions. Sure, there were no more wars or murders, but love, passion, and creativity faded away as well. Beauty and the gift and comfort of music disappeared. Before long, people could no longer distinguish between colors; everything from an apple to the sky was the same bland hue. The messiness and mayhem of life were removed for the sake of a safe, but mundane and monotone, existence.

The main character, Jonas, an inquisitive sixteen-year-old, comes to realize, through various encounters with an old man, the "Receiver of Memories," what the community is missing. He is able to see vividly and experience every memory the old man has. As a result, Jonas changes. He becomes determined to restore the full gamut of human emotional experience to the community. Although Jonas dodges death many times along the way, he heroically accomplishes his goal by the end of the movie.

Perhaps there are times you might like to align yourselves with the elders of *The Giver* and eradicate those bothersome emotions. The truth is, without them your existence would be dull, boring, lifeless, and loveless. Emotions are God-given and vital to being human. They are the music to the unchoreographed dance of life. Knowing how to name them and tame them in Jesus's name, without inflaming them and aiming them at others, makes life a whole lot more intelligible and enjoyable.

CHAPTER 4

Shock Absorbers

Mental pain is less dramatic than physical pain, but it is more common and also more hard to bear. The frequent attempt to conceal mental pain increases the burden: it is easier to say "My tooth is aching" than to say "My heart is broken."
—C. S. LEWIS, *The Problem of Pain*

Desperate to experience the full goodness of God, Moses cried out to God, "Now show me your glory" (Exod. 33:18–20). Ironically, if God had done as Moses asked, one can only assume the fiery glory of God's holiness would have burned a hole right through Moses's eyes, fried his brain, and disintegrated him right where he stood. Moses's request was naively dangerous, like having the item "stand ten feet away from the sun and take a selfie" on your bucket list. Not a good idea. So in great love and mercy, instead of striking Moses dead right where he stood, God said to him, "You cannot see my face, for no one may see me and live." God chose to reveal his back instead of his face. God loved Moses; he didn't give him what he wanted but, rather, what he could handle.

Just as humans would crumble, die, and disintegrate in the presence of such *goodness*, we suffer similar negative consequences through excessive *badness*, otherwise known as *trauma*.

God originally created us with perfect hardware and software designed to lovingly and intimately connect with himself, creation, and others—not to live through much of the brutal violence, loss, and other kinds of trauma we experience throughout our lives. Even though human beings are resilient and can weather the most brutal of circumstances, many of us can be crushed by the weight of certain traumatic events.

Trauma comes from a Greek word meaning "wound" or "injury." Traumatic events can cause various degrees of injury to our souls that affect our physiology, spirituality, and relationality. For most people, a traumatic event disrupts the God-given emotional GPS and causes it to go bonkers, resulting in overpowering emotions, ruminating thoughts, and even painful sensations in the body. Our unique individual trauma tolerance is determined by our upbringing, the level of safe support we currently have, our temperament, and our current level of life stressors.

Heartbreak affects everyone differently. For some, heartbreak is big *T* trauma, while others experience it as little *t* trauma. One thing is for sure: heartbreak is one of the most painful experiences on earth.

No matter to what degree one has experienced the trauma of heartbreak, there is a common psychological tactic people use to deal with the overwhelming emotions and negative thoughts, and that is to engage stealthy shock absorbers. As we will see, these shock absorbers, commonly known as defense mechanisms, can be helpful in the short-term but destructive in the long-term.

Shock Absorbers

Do you know about the *shocks* on your car? Shocks absorb dangerous energy from bumps and potholes in the road so that the rough terrain and bouncing up and down does not destroy the vehicle. They also help the driver maintain control of the car when faced with an unexpected jolt. The greater the energy, the more the shock absorbers work to absorb it.

Shock absorbers in cars are similar to our wired-in emotional and psychological shock absorbers, otherwise known as defense mechanisms. Our defenses are innate gifts to us sometimes-frail people who are unable to fully experience the debilitating and devastating blows to our souls.

In the aftermath of a devastating romantic breakup, for example, the intensity of the experience can be too difficult for us to allow into our conscious awareness. So rather than coming into contact with and absorbing the negative and painful energy, our inner shock absorbers take it and redirect it somewhere else. Let's look at some examples.

Denial

One of the most common shock absorbers is denial, which is usually disguised as rationalization (making excuses). I asked my clients what they thought when their partners initially broke up with them:

"Yeah, right! This is not happening to me."

"You've got to be kidding. This is a joke, right?"

"Even though my girlfriend is saying no, I know God will work on her heart and change her mind."

"I am a good Christian, so God would never allow me to experience this kind of pain."

"No, you are not breaking up with me. I have put too much time and effort into this relationship."

"Just give it some time; we will work through it."

Some people knew the breakup was coming and still said some of these things. Shock absorbers allow us to dip a toe in the river of pain instead of jumping in headfirst. They are all unconscious ways people deny reality so they won't be overwhelmed by the terror of loss.

People can remain in denial for a very long time after a breakup. I was in denial for about a year after my girlfriend dumped me. I couldn't let her go. I thought maybe she needed space, time to see that she really loved me. Even after she rekindled her relationship with her ex-boyfriend, I still held out hope. "She loves me; she will be back," I said to myself. My denial kept the reality of the loss from crushing me and redirected my energy toward the fantasy of her coming back. But then, eventually, for my own sake and sanity, I had to let go (we will talk more about letting go in a later chapter).

Splitting

Splitting is a defense that causes heartbroken people to see others as either good or bad to keep the painful reality of the situation and the difficult emotions from entering their awareness. Splitting also enables people to steer away from complex feelings of ambivalence, which are often uncomfortable. It is sometimes easier to see the world as black and white than it is to see it in shades of gray.

For example, angry totalizing statements, such as, "He is a piece of garbage. He doesn't deserve me," or "It's all his fault. He is going to hell for what he did," or "I am glad she broke up with me; she was a loser anyway," are all attempts to *split* ex-partners as all bad, in an attempt to soften the blow of the breakup and feel better about themselves. If their ex is all bad, then they are all good. This is in contrast to a more balanced and truthful perspective in seeing the good and opportunities for growth in both themselves and their ex-partner.

Also, the heartbroken tend to split their exes as all bad to avoid their ambivalent feelings of love toward them. It is easier to hate them, or at the very least evaluate them negatively, than to be honest with themselves that they are conflicted—they have feelings of both love and hate toward their ex. There is research to suggest that those who harbor negative evaluations of their ex-partner directly after a breakup "show superior post-break-up emotional adjustment."[1] Like all defense mechanisms, splitting serves an adaptive purpose, although what might be helpful initially can become a hindrance to overall well-being later on.

The Blame Game

Another common shock absorber is blaming. This one is an oldie. Remember Adam and Eve in the book of Genesis? Even though they both ate the forbidden fruit, they hid from God (a type of denial) because of their deep sense of shame. The only problem was, it is difficult to play hide-and-seek with the creator of the universe. So, when God found them, Adam engaged the shock absorber of blame.

> And he [God] said . . . "Have you eaten from the tree that I commanded you not to eat from?"
> The man said, "The woman you put here with me—she gave me some fruit from the tree, and I ate it." . . .
> The woman said, "The serpent deceived me." (3:11–13)

Adam and Eve could not allow themselves to be fully exposed and take responsibility for what they had done. Perhaps their individual pain and shame were so intense that they chose to blame in order to get the loving, penetrating gaze of God off of themselves and onto someone else.

This type of blaming is common after a breakup. One partner says, "It's your fault! If only you hadn't . . ." And then the other partner interrupts and yells, "Well, you promised . . . And if only *you* hadn't . . ." And around and around they go.

Attacking

Blaming usually goes hand in hand with attacking, another common defense mechanism. Cursing and slandering one another are different forms of attack and are meant to absorb the shock of emotional pain and direct it elsewhere. Those who are heartbroken and overtaken by anger can use an attack defense as a distraction to keep from feeling the pain and loss of the relationship.

One common example of attacking is when partners text verbal missiles to one another. Though it has been many years since my breakup, I remember thinking countless times about what my ex did to me—and feeling so much pain, pain that quickly turned to deep anger. To distract myself from the heartache, I took my weapons (my thumbs) and fired a barrage of hurtful texts at my ex-girlfriend. I wanted her to suffer as much as I had. Then I felt bad about the angry texts and apologized, only to do it again a few days later.

In the immediacy of a breakup, strict logic tends to fly out the window, and as a result, I allowed pain, reactivity, and defense mechanisms to take the reins in everything I said and did. I reacted out of hurt and used the defenses of attacking and blaming to cover up my pain, which included my terror of abandonment and fear of perpetual loneliness (which existed way before my relationship with her). I simply did not have the mature and healthy thinking, reacting, communication, and coping skills that I do now.

Years later, I look back and realize our breakup was not all my ex's fault. I was not exactly a mature guy making all the right decisions in the relationship. I had to own my part and needed to be honest with the emotional, relational, and spiritual immaturity I brought into the relationship. Also, she was entitled to make any decision she wanted for her future; there were no laws or contracts binding us together. Those were difficult lessons to learn.

External Shock Absorbers

External—or what I call run-and-numb—shock absorbers are commonly used by people experiencing heartbreak. For example, many people run to drugs and alcohol to numb their pain. Others run to pornography to get a rush and distract themselves from loneliness, sadness, and grief. Still others run quickly into the arms of another lover to feel powerful or to receive assurance that someone finds them desirable or lovable. Some people become workaholics, laboring longer and longer hours. Finally, some read the Bible for hours a day, go on as many mission trips as they can, and hide their pain under the guise of religiosity. These are all false intimacies and distractions that help people numb their pain and loss.

Shock Absorbers: They Help and Hinder

Let's say you are the mutant Multiple Man, a fictional character from the Marvel Universe who has the ability to duplicate himself (he appeared in *X-Men: The Last Stand*). He can split off into one, five, ten, or more carbon copies of himself. At some later point the duplicates are absorbed back into the original Multiple Man.

Now think of the duplicates as your shock absorbers, or defense mechanisms. Let's say you're in an epic battle with an alien (breaking up), who is shooting a harmful, large-diameter radiation gun at you (trauma). So you employ one of your duplicates (defenses) to jump in front of you and absorb the radiation. Even though the original you has been saved, your duplicate has absorbed the energy. The problem is that after doing their jobs, the duplicates (defenses) reenter you and inevitably contaminate you and anyone in relationship with you. Defenses are necessary to protect you, but at some point they become hazardous to your health.

In many ways, shock absorbers are like helpful friends, seeking to be a blessing. They have a good agenda and try to look out for your best interests and make sure you do not become overwhelmed. While shock absorbers, like medications, can bring enormous benefits to your physical and emotional health, they can also produce disastrous side effects. Even though shock absorbers help you cope with the aftermath of trauma and loss—keeping your anxiety, emotions, and pain at bay—they can also hinder the grieving process, which over time can negatively affect you and those in relationship with you.

For example, let's say that you use the shock absorbers of work and alcohol to deal with the intense pain of your heartbreak. Despite being maladaptive defenses, they do help you get by and not become completely overwhelmed with and debilitated by negative emotions. The problem is that you numb out with work and alcohol so often that you don't have time for meaningful relationships, and you wind up pushing away those who really want to help you. At some point, you will need to let go of the defenses so you can live and love in a healthier way.

Take heart; thanks to our ancient ancestors Adam and Eve, we have all learned how to sew fig leaves together to make coverings for our fragile and hurting soul. It is a wired-in process that typically happens outside our awareness, just like breathing. Even the best of saints have used shock absorbers to deal with emotional pain.

King David's Shock Absorber

King David suffered some major traumatic experiences. He went from being a shepherd to being a warrior king, in a relatively short period of time. He fought in numerous military campaigns and experienced the horror and savagery of war. At times, he feared for his life as he hid from the jealous and murderous rage of King Saul. Some of his family members and fellow soldiers betrayed him. If that wasn't enough, God busted him for having an affair; because of his sin, his dear child died. Talk about drama, trauma, and pain.

Is it possible he had post-traumatic stress disorder (PTSD)? Do you think he suffered to such a great extent emotionally that he needed some run-and-numb shock absorbers? Anyone who has been through what David went through might have some emotional issues. I think David, the man after God's own heart, used sex, sinfully, as a shock absorber to deal with his emotional pain because of the trauma and loss.

Let's look at some evidence. Although most commentators would say David's victory dance and disrobing in front of his slave girls (2 Sam. 6:20) was a sacred and pure act, I am a little suspicious. That is at least a red flag in my book. The real glaring evidence of his shock-absorbing tendencies is found in 2 Samuel 11:2–4. When he was lazily walking around one evening, he spotted Bathsheba and decided he had to have her. It was lust at first sight. Even though he had no idea what kind of person she was, he had an insatiable urge to have sex with her. He didn't care that she was a married woman. He had his messengers drag her from her home, and, "she came to him, and he slept with her." He then ordered her husband killed so he could have her all to himself. I suspect what he did with Bathsheba was probably not his first rodeo. We do know that David had a bunch of other wives and concubines (glorified sex slaves).

What the heck?

A man after God's own heart?

You've got to be kidding me!

But according to God's Word, he was.

Remember, being a man or woman after God's own heart never means perfection. It has to do with direction more than anything else. No matter what sin King David committed, he eventually wound up on his knees begging for God's mercy and forgiveness.

To be fair, David lived in a very different time than we do. Kings in power typically had many wives (polygamy) and concubines. Nobody knows how aware or unaware King David was of God's revelation concerning monogamy (being married to one person). But lying, murder, adultery? Well, that is a different story. King David knew better.

It is possible that God tried to nudge him toward monogamy, truthfulness, and faithfulness during moments of prayer, but David's emotional pain from past experiences and his lustful shock absorber were much too compelling.

The consequences of David's defense mechanism greatly affected not only his own life but also the lives of generations after him. Richard Rohr, an internationally known Franciscan friar, writes, "If you do not transform your pain, you will surely transmit it to those around you and even to the next generation."[2] David probably passed down his shock-absorbing tendency toward sexual sin to his son Solomon. And Solomon magnified it exponentially, for 1 Kings 11:3 says, "He had seven hundred wives of royal birth and three hundred concubines, and his wives led him astray."

Unfortunately, if we sow defenses we will eventually reap expenses. There is always a cost associated with sinful coping mechanisms. King David and King Solomon eventually found that out the hard way. We will too.

Using shock absorbers to cope with your heartbreak is understandable. It is part of the grieving process. I am not saying it is the best way to grieve, but if we were all honest, it is what we do as broken and wounded human beings.

Instead of using shock absorbers—defense mechanisms—we need to face the pain, uncomfortable emotions, and distressing thoughts head-on and use God-ordained coping strategies. We can become more aware of the defenses we use and do something different. We will look at how to do that in more detail in part III of this book, especially in the chapter titled, "Heal: Deal, Feel, Reveal, Seal (DFRS)."

I offer you sincere compassion in this trying time. Heartbreak is hard. Through God's grace and your daily intention to grieve well, you will be less prone to using destructive defense mechanisms and learn valuable life lessons along the way.

CHAPTER 5

The Door Is Closing

All the art of living lies in a fine mingling
of letting go and holding on.
—HENRY ELLIS

G loria dated Carl for about two years before he broke up
with her to be with her best friend. For about a year after
the breakup, she hated him. She seethed with anger even at the
mere mention of his name. Every chance she got, she let people
know what a jerk he was for breaking up with her and leaving
her for "that bimbo." Gloria could not understand why God
would bring Carl into her life if he knew Carl would hurt her
the way he did. She suffered from insomnia, something she had
never struggled with before, and experienced stomach problems
and frequent headaches.

Gloria's journey toward a healed heart and peaceful acceptance was long and hard. With work and time, Gloria experienced deep changes in her character and shifted her perception of
Carl, herself, the breakup, and God. Little by little, she integrated
new information into her awareness that even changed how she
remembered some events. Neuroscience research now demonstrates that memories can be altered and updated (it's called
memory reconsolidation)[1] and that was exactly what Gloria was

experiencing. Gloria was able to differentiate between what Carl had done, which was a wrongful act of betrayal, and who he was, which was a flawed human being, just like her.

Through Gloria's grieving practices, such as contemplative prayer and journaling, she recognized inner wounds that perpetuated long-held patterns of distrust in God, addiction to food, and bitterness toward her parents as a result of early childhood trauma. With integration ultimately comes transformation: As Gloria allowed God to compassionately reveal and heal her inner wounds with grace, healing, and forgiveness, she experienced more empathy for Carl. And as she experienced greater degrees of integration, her physical symptoms of anxiety, insomnia, and stomach problems dissipated.

It took Gloria about a year to grieve well. She processed her anger; endured a time of sadness and fear; forgave her ex, her best friend, and even God; and became vulnerable by allowing herself to be loved again. Gloria was able to come to a place of acceptance, "forget the former things," "not dwell on the past," and embrace the new things God was doing in her life (Isa. 43:18–19). There is a common myth that says if you divide the amount of time you were in the relationship by half, that is a good estimate for how long it will take to fully recover from a broken heart.[2] That estimation fits in Gloria's case, but it is different for everybody. In reality, it takes as long as it takes.

Acceptance

The last leg of the grieving journey involves experiencing deeper surrender and acceptance and closing the door of your heart to your ex. It is a time of ceasing to bargain for the relationship. In other words, you no longer try to earn God's favor through extensive prayer and sin management hoping to convince him you and your ex are made for each other, and you don't try to persuade your ex to come back by sending text messages promising that you have changed. Acceptance is an attitude that doesn't get stuck in the past, fret about the future, or fight for a different outcome; it embraces the present, with all of its guts and glory.

Integration

When a person comes to a place of acceptance, which is the last stage of the grieving process, he or she has experienced integration. Integration occurs when the different complex parts of the narrative surrounding the breakup, including your role, your ex's, and God's, come together as a whole.

It is almost as if the logical left-brain and the emotional right-brain have discussed the events and come to a friendly agreement on the who, what, when, where, why, and how of the breakup. Events that were cloudy and chaotic now seem clear and meaningful. Anxiety-fueled questions—such as, Where were you, God? and Why did you allow this to happen to me?—are no longer front and center. The person who has walked well through the shadowy depths of grief is able to find God's grace and peace in the midst of what was once perceived as a godless tragedy.

Additionally, where there is integration, there is no longer a need for defense mechanisms such as denial, splitting, blaming, and attacking. The person who has grieved well no longer sees the ex as the evil enemy, who is 100 percent to blame for everything, and no longer sees him- or herself as the perfect partner, who always did everything right. The heartbroken person is able to see the brokenness that might have contributed to the breakup in both parties. They are finally able to ask with a surrendered and hopeful heart, "Okay, God, what plans do you have for me next?"

Abuse and Betrayal Are Not Your Fault

My discussion of integration and looking inward can trigger deep anger for any who feel I am blaming them for the events that led to the breakup. Because of my work with many women and men who have experienced domestic violence and other forms of abuse, I can say that it is never in any way your fault that you were abused. The fact that I am advocating prayerful self-reflection as a means to understanding a breakup does not mean I am saying you deserved to be betrayed, demeaned, or devalued. It is never your fault when another person uses their own free will to sin against you.

Self-reflection and integration are not about blame; rather, they are about a journey through prayer that results in deep understanding. This understanding leads to future life change in a more positive direction. Being able to see the good, the bad, the beautiful, and the ugly within ourselves and others through compassionate eyes is difficult, but it can be profoundly rewarding. My hope is that you will reflect on the relationship, from the start all the way through to the bitter end, and gain valuable insights that will help you with any relationship you might have in the future.

The Sting Is Gone

Have you ever been stung by a bee? Those beautiful yet pesky creatures, buzzing around, looking for some yummy nectar to slurp, can pack quite a wallop. I know; I have been stung by one, and it hurts! While most people who get stung usually have acute pain, a small red welt, and slight swelling (your immune system trying to fight foreign invaders), some people have an extreme, severe reaction, which can be life-threatening. Once the stinger is removed, a dab of hydrocortisone will reduce the swelling and the healing can begin. At some point all of the soreness, redness, and swelling will be gone, and the bee sting will be a thing of the past. Some people take a day to fully heal; others take up to a week. Everyone is different.

If you have grieved well, you will no longer feel deep pain and anguish when thoughts of your ex come buzzing around in your brain. The well of tears will have dried up. Over time, love from God and others will act like hydrocortisone and reduce the soreness and aching in your heart. Love from God and others will not be your only source of healing. Just as there is a God-given innate mechanism that will bring healing to the body after a bee sting, so there is an innate mechanism that will bring healing to your soul after a breakup. Some psychologists refer to that innate motivational impulse toward ever increasing growth and expansion as "transformance,"[3] and others simply as the power of the persevering human spirit. Eventually, through different sources of strength and love, you will heal. The wound will finally scar over and will no longer be sensitive to touch. You will finally be able to close the door of your heart and say good-bye to your ex. The sting of heartbreak will be gone.

Remember, It's a Process

You might experience moments in your journey when you think you've said good riddance to the zigzag and you're positive the door is bolted shut, but a thunderous wind suddenly blows it open and catapults you onto the Montu roller coaster for one last ride. Life is messy, and so is the grieving process.

A Grief Observed by C. S. Lewis, a famous theologian and apologist, is a brutally honest account of Lewis's own painful grieving process after losing his wife, as recorded through his journal entries. At one point, he even wrestled with whether or not God is a "cosmic sadist," someone who enjoys inflicting pain on others. In the following excerpt, Lewis recorded a time when the door of grief blasted open and took him by surprise, revealing that he was not as far along in the grieving process as he thought:

> Tonight all the hells of young grief have opened again; the mad words, the bitter resentment, the fluttering in the stomach, the nightmare unreality, the wallowed-in tears. For in grief nothing "stays put." One keeps on emerging from a phase, but it always recurs. Round and round. Everything repeats. Am I going in circles, or dare I hope I am on a spiral?[4]

Remember, the grieving process is not like a straight line but more like a lightning bolt, full of unpredictable zigzags. You can feel that you have fully integrated the breakup, feel a degree of wholeness, and then the door of grief might fling open wide, when you least expect it. As painful as that oftentimes intrusive experience can be, it is just a sign that God has more healing work to do within you.

The Door Is Closed

Fully grieving the loss of your ex means coming to a place of acceptance. It means the door of your heart naturally closes to the other person and you no longer feel the need to forcefully slam it shut and place a double-reinforced, stainless-steel padlock on it. One day, you wake up and find the door shut, naturally. The mention of your ex's name doesn't bring intense anxiety, a lump in your throat, and a knot in your stomach. You can hear his or her name and remember what you went through, but the agonizing sting is gone, and you can, with a prayer, wish your ex well on his or her journey. Acceptance is the *last* stage of the grieving process. You are probably reading this in the beginning of your grieving process. Take heart and give it some time; that moment will come.

PART II

Grieving Pathways

So far, we have discussed the common complexities and nuances associated with the grieving process following a breakup. I hope it has enhanced your understanding of your own journey and has helped you feel less alone, crazy, and confused. I realize that, if your heart has been broken, you don't want a mere description; you want a prescription, or practical solutions to help you heal, be transformed, and move forward. This next section looks at healing pathways of connection that will be instrumental for your grieving journey and, ultimately, for the rest of your life.

Unlike the typical crosses we see in churches in the West, the historic Lorraine Cross has two horizontal crossbeams and one long vertical beam. Although there are several interpretations of the design that point to the work of Christ on the cross, for me the *design also symbolizes the threefold relational pathways essential to the grieving process:*

1. *The vertical pathway symbolizes the relationship we need with God.*

2. *The first horizontal pathway symbolizes the relationship we need with others and creation.*

3. *The second horizontal pathway symbolizes the relationship we need with ourselves.*

The degree to which we are lovingly connected to the vertical and horizontal pathways is the degree to which we will experience emotional and spiritual health and vitality. One without the others leaves a lopsided faith and a grieving process that loses out on valuable relational resources for healing and transformation. In part II, each chapter will focus on a specific relational pathway—with God, others, and ourselves—while examining obstacles that can block those paths.

CHAPTER 6

The Vertical Pathway
(Connection with God)

You, God, are my God, earnestly I seek you;
I thirst for you, my whole being longs for you,
in a dry and parched land where there is no water.

—PSALM 63:1

In Matthew 22:36, an inquisitive legal expert regarding religious matters asked Jesus, "Which is the greatest commandment in the Law?" In other words, for those of us who profess to believe and trust in almighty God, what is our priority in this life?

Jesus answered boldly and without hesitation, "Love doctrines and debating, judging, and condemning others with all your heart, soul, strength, and mind."

Oops, I am sorry! I was quoting from the Legalistic Religious Bible. Forgive me; that is not the version I wanted to quote from. Jesus really said, "'Love the Lord your God with all your heart and with all your soul and with all your mind.' This is the first and greatest commandment. And the second is like it: 'Love your neighbor as yourself'" (Matt. 22:37–39).

The greatest of all the commandments (and there are a lot of them) is an order to love with all your being. Throughout history, God has always shouted through a megaphone that life is all about vibrant and intimate relationships that last into eternity. It is time to get cross-eyed and connect with the threefold relational pathways that are going to help you get through your grieving process. This chapter will focus on the vertical pathway, which emphasizes your relationship with God.

The Vertical Pathway

Fostering intimacy and connection with God during our time in the dry and weary land of grief is as smart as sending your iPhone to Apple for repair. Just as Apple is the manufacturer of your iPhone and knows its ins and outs and complex intricacies, God is the creator (manufacturer) of you, and he thoroughly knows and loves you. So just as Apple is able to repair your iPhone, God is able to repair your heart.

Let's do an exercise. Note any thoughts or emotions that arise within you when you read these next few sentences. Ready? Here we go.

God loves you.

No, really. God really, really does love you.

God wants to tenderly hold you and comfort you during this difficult time.

God is good, and you can trust him with all your heart.

What is your gut reaction? Can you take those words in? Do they bring comfort? Do they make you angry? Do you feel indifferent? Do you have thoughts like, *Amen, I am so grateful that he does.* Or do you have thoughts like, *Yeah, right. God is the one who did this to me.* Perhaps you're wondering, *God holding me, comforting me—what does that look or feel like?*

There are many different types of responses people have to the above questions. There are no right or wrong answers. It is an exercise that allows you to gauge where your wounded heart is with God in the midst of your season of heartbreak. After having their hearts broken some people angrily move further away from God, while some draw closer for loving comfort. Some people feel guilty because they no longer feel free to tell others how wonderful and amazing God is because it feels as if God has abandoned them. And while others don't feel that God has abandoned them, praying seems like a monumental enterprise. Once you know how you feel toward God, it provides a clue to the areas in your life to which God can bring growth and healing.

I admit that I am biased. I want your answers to point toward a dynamic relationship with God. It saddens me, and I am sure it also saddens God, that his beloved children run *from* him in the midst of adversity, brokenness, and pain, instead of running *to* him. I also understand that life is messy, our faith gets tested, and the best of saints have dark nights of the soul. Wherever you are with God, the key is to be honest about it and to be open to experiencing his tenderness, love, and affirmation in a profoundly tangible way during your season of heartbreak.

Obstacles to God

Although we logically know how vitally important it is to stay connected to God in our grieving journey, sometimes debris can block our paths toward God. I want to talk about two important obstacles that typically keep people from a loving relationship with God during a season of heartbreak. One has to do with overwhelming emotions, and the other has to do with a person's "soul wear," or internal image of God.

Overwhelming Emotions

My nieces and nephews are adorable. Normally, they are well mannered and well behaved, but they also have moments when they are out of control. Some days when I visit my brother, they are running wildly around the house, shrieking loudly, throwing things at their siblings, and refusing to listen to reason. During these times, I ask my brother, half-jokingly, if they have had a mound of candy. He usually says yes.

The kids are having what is called a sugar rush. Although, anecdotally, some researchers claim the phenomenon is bogus, it definitely seems real in my nieces and nephews.[1] They eat some delicious candy and the sugar rushes through their bloodstreams, then their cells start doing the happy dance and they can't sit still. Even when my brother or I tell them to settle down and sit on the couch like good little boys and girls, they continue to squirm and make weird animal noises, and one of them invariably gets in trouble for hitting another.

One reason that people going through a breakup find it difficult to sit still and pray is that they are flooded with a rush of swirling emotions—much like my nieces and nephews when they're experiencing the wacky effects of sugar in the bloodstream. From a brain-science perspective, the bomb of the breakup has exploded and activated the heartbroken person's *sympathetic* threat system, putting him or her in fight-or-flight mode. The person is flooded with intense emotion that propels him or her to move and take action. That emotional energy can cause a person to feel anxious, making it extremely hard to be still and pray.

The person not only can't sit still because of their emotional energy, but he or she doesn't want to sit still. He or she is unconsciously afraid that the difficult emotions and negative thoughts will rise to the surface and become unbearable. In other words, sitting still means facing the anger, shame, sadness, and fear brought on by heartbreak, and many people would prefer a rain check instead, or even better, to lose the receipt.

Some people, however, have a secure attachment (emotionally connected relationship) with God and can discipline and regulate their emotions and unwanted thoughts enough to sit and be soothed by his presence. Through prayer, they can feel the delight of their triggered *parasympathetic* nervous system—the God-designed calming system of the body. Usually, these people have prayed through emotional pain often enough in the past that it has become an ingrained automatic spiritual discipline.

But I totally get it if you struggle to pray during extremely emotional and difficult times. Your intense emotions and activated sympathetic nervous system, the part of you that wakes you up, energizes you, and prepares you to fight or flee, kicks into high gear. It then seems impossible for you to sit in silence. Ask God to help you calm down and pray. Try it for thirty seconds for one day, then one minute, then five minutes, then back to three minutes if it gets too difficult. Adjust accordingly until you are able to pray for longer periods of time with ease.

I had an insecure attachment style of relating to God (and other people), which in simple terms means I had a hard time trusting that God is good and cares deeply for me. Initially, when I experienced the devastating loss of my girlfriend, I had to distract myself with graduate work, movies, hanging out with friends, getting into another relationship, and even doing busy leadership work for God. Stillness was scary for me. Being quiet with God was like looking into an ultra-clear and streak-free glass mirror; it was terrifying. In God's presence, my brokenness with all its painful emotions and pessimistic thoughts about myself and the future became crystal clear, but at the time, I was not ready for the intensity.

Thank God, I learned the practice of being in the beautifully dangerous presence of God. Although it was dangerous, as there was no telling what dark, painful, or challenging experience would be revealed and encountered in the light of God's love, it was also beautiful because the God I had been running from was far more loving, gentle, and supportive than I ever imagined. God's ability to tenderly show truth without overwhelming me helped me trust him more as time passed, and it helped me move from an insecure attachment to a secure attachment with him.

If you are struggling to experience a relational pathway with God because of overwhelming emotions, know that others are in the same boat. Even Jesus's disciples struggled with praying, which is why they asked Jesus to teach them how to pray (Luke 11:1). When you ask the same, from an earnest and broken heart, God will have compassion and help you.

Intense emotions are not the only obstacle that can keep heartbroken people in pain and feeling separated from the presence of a loving God. The biggest obstacle I have encountered in pastoral ministry and in counseling clients experiencing grief is their soul wear, their internalized image of who they think God is.

Soul Wear

Eyewear comes in all shapes and sizes, with radical and colorful lens and frame choices, and in a variety of prescriptions. Some dramatically affect how you see the world. There are glasses you can wear to see the world in a reddish or bluish tint. You can put on glasses that give you a glimpse of how a person who is nearly blind sees the world, or you can experience a virtual tour through the eyes of a person with dementia. There are even glasses that you can wear to see how bees see the world. I and countless others would be blind—unable to see the world in all its beautiful complexity—without glasses. They are truly a godsend.

Just as we have eyewear, we have what I call soul wear, the unique lens our soul wears when it views God, the world, and ourselves. Some people wear darkly tinted soul wear. To them the world appears unsafe, neither God nor people can be trusted. Some people wear rose-colored soul wear and perceive reality as better than it really is. Each person's soul wear is uniquely shaped by one's life experiences.

Although research shows that our relationships with caregivers in our first few years of development are the most important, other crucial dynamics shape how we see the world as well.[2] A person's place of birth, ethnicity, culture, temperament, and socioeconomic background—along with national crises such as war, financial collapse, or racial or ethnic instability—all play a part in forming his or her soul wear. That is why there are so many unique perspectives about God and the world we live in.

The blessing of soul wear is that there are so many fun, creative, and exciting ways to see the world. The curse is that our soul wear can be shaped in such a way that it distorts reality, becomes an obstacle, and negatively affects how we relate to God, others, and ourselves.

Do you struggle to trust God? If I asked you whether God is primarily angry, sad, or glad toward you, what would be your core response? Is your perception of God laced with criticism, harshness, or judgment? When was the last time you heard God say he loves you or is proud of you? In the midst of grief, are you more prone to worship God with your intellect, yet find your heart and emotions cut off or cold toward him? Or do you feel God's presence, enjoy his holy hugs, and hold on to him for dear life?

Your responses to these questions are directly related to your soul wear. Soul wear makes it either quite easy or extremely difficult to love God and to let him love you. Let me share a couple of examples.

Mariah's Soul Wear

Mariah was a spunky young woman at my church. She grew up in an urban neighborhood with safe, hardworking, and loving parents. They were not rich, but they seldom had to worry about affording rent or food. They were far from perfect, but Mariah always felt safe enough to confide in them and seek advice when she was in trouble. If she got hurt, she knew her parents would provide a listening ear, along with empathy, comfort, safety, and encouragement.

Mariah's soul wear was largely shaped by her relationship with her amazing parents. For her it was a no-brainer to go to God with the grief she experienced when she broke up with her fiancé, because her parents had always loved and comforted her. Mariah internalized that care and comfort, which shaped her soul wear, so she saw God as the loving, comforting, healing God that he is. Breaking up with her fiancé was definitely one of the worst times of her life, but she was able to grieve well and find tremendous strength and comfort in God's presence because she experienced God as a safe haven. Unfortunately, not everyone is as blessed as Mariah.

My Soul Wear

My soul wear was quite different from Mariah's, though also largely shaped by my family environment and social relationships. I think most families are dysfunctional to some degree, but my family's level of dysfunction was off the charts. My parents divorced when I was six. My mom had been a drug addict for as long as I can remember; she eventually passed away from an overdose when I was in my mid twenties. My relationship with my dad was strained while I was growing up, but I am thankful that has wonderfully changed over the years. On a brighter note, as I look back, I am greatly appreciative of some loving aunts, uncles, and grandparents.

Relationships with my peers were also very important in shaping my lenses. My peers made fun of and picked on me incessantly for wearing Coke-bottle glasses. They called me a *nerd* before the word came to mean someone smart who could, potentially, make millions of dollars, like Bill Gates. I was always the last kid picked for gym class team activities. In addition to having difficult relationships, I was a sensitive young kid by nature (temperament) and someone who internalized all my pain, abuse, neglect, and abandonment.

My inner lenses had a darker tint, and I looked at the world in a less-trusting way than Mariah did. I had deep abandonment issues, along with powerful, engrained, lie-based inner beliefs etched on my soul. I believed, mostly on an unconscious level, that I couldn't count on anyone—that no one would ever really love me for who I was, and that men in authority disliked me and were always angry with me. And guess what? I projected all those distortions onto God during my painful season of heartbreak.

Now don't get me wrong. I loved God and had a relationship with him, but deep pain triggered some lie-based emotional perspectives and kept me from experiencing God's love and comfort when I really needed him the most. I didn't want to hang out with a God who didn't like me, who criticized me, and who was too masculine to show me compassion, affection, and tenderness. I was in desperate need of a soul makeover.

It's Not Your Fault, But . . .

I now realize that my experiences were valid and my inability to come to God with the open-armed, simple faith of a child made sense. To a large extent, I didn't fashion or design my soul wear. My impaired vision was not my fault. My lenses looked an awful lot like those worn by previous generations of my family members. It is also not your fault if you have painful hurts and traumas from childhood that get in the way of your intimacy with God and of relating to other people confidently. Believe me when I say this, God can and will give you a new prescription.

It can also be difficult when you believe God loves you if it doesn't feel like he does. Research from cutting-edge neuroscience (science that looks at the nervous system and brain) now shows that *head* knowledge (explicit knowledge), which is based in one part of the brain, is different from *heart* knowledge (implicit knowledge), based in another part of the brain.[3] In other words, it makes sense that we sing, "Jesus loves me—this I know, for the Bible tells me so" from our heads, yet sing contradictory lie-based verses like, "Jesus loves them, but not me, because I am so dirty" from our hearts.

If it seems you have multiple personalities when it comes to your faith, rest assured, you are not crazy. Science validates our experience and shows us that two different regions of the brain can be thinking contradictory thoughts at the same time. The hope is that we can combine and integrate our head knowledge with our heart knowledge and align them with the truth of who God says we are and who he really is. Through hard work (engagement in spiritual disciplines) and God's grace (compassionate love), it can be done.

As adults, it is our responsibility to do something about the pair of lenses we were given as children. We can either go to SoulCrafters and allow God, the skilled Ophthalmologist, to begin the work of enhancing our vision or stick with our own fogged-up lenses that have been shaped by pain. While we need to acknowledge our past, we do not have to allow it to dictate our present and future. We can either remain victims of our circumstances or become victors who take hold, through God's Spirit, of all he has planned for us.

LASIK

LASIK is an amazing surgery that uses a laser to reshape a person's cornea, allowing light to enter in just the right way to help correct someone's vision. In this section, I want to share powerful Spirit-inspired truths from Scripture to correct your vision of who God is. A spiritual LASIK procedure, if you will. I hope to modify your soul wear and remove unnecessary obstacles to allow your heart's eye to more readily recognize the God of love. I also want to offer some healthy images that, when embraced, can help you transition into prayer with greater ease during this difficult time of your life. I don't think I can get you to 20/20, but I do think I can sharpen your heart's vision by a few degrees.

Images of God

What is your internal image of God during your season of grief? Or during times when you feel beaten up by the effects of sin, whether someone else's or your own? When you are tired, dirty, lost, confused, scared, hungry, and desperate, how do you think God views you? What do you think God wants to say to you or do in those moments?

Is God like a tough drill sergeant, demanding that you give him twenty push-ups for failing at another relationship? Is God a wise Yoda, teaching you lessons for your journey? Is he a prosecutor, pointing out every mistake you made along the way? Is God a distant uncle who loves you even though you haven't heard from him or seen him in a while? Humans have many unhelpful ways of relating to God that don't paint a full or accurate picture of who he is.

While the ancient contemplatives, such as the psalmists, had a more intimate picture of God, the Israelites' primary view of God emphasized that he is *holy*—God is totally separated from sin and completely different from everything that exists. The Hebrews never wrote the name of God in the Scriptures. They used only the sacred letters YHWH, leaving out the vowels, in an attempt to preserve the "otherness" of the living God. Any Israelite caught pronouncing the name of God was stoned to death. It was whispered only once a year when the high priest, with incense and candles, went into the Holy of Holies and lay prostrate on the ground.[4]

At the time Jesus walked the earth, the Greek philosophers—the most prominent of whom were the Stoics—greatly affected the mind-set of people all over Europe and the Roman Empire. They saw God as unemotional, incapable of feeling or relating to emotion. This idea of God was very important during that time, however, because a God who had feelings could easily be subdued by them. The Stoics considered this to be too vulnerable and belittling to be true of a holy God. Unfortunately, tainted and defective soul wear greatly affected many people's view of God at the time.

God as Abba

Jesus was familiar with the many different metaphors and images used to describe God in Scripture. In Exodus 15:3, Moses wrote, "The LORD is a warrior." Other Old Testament writers described God as Healer, Lord, Rock, Fortress, Lover, Stronghold, Lion, Leopard, Shepherd, Groom, Potter, Judge, Pillar of Cloud, Wind, Fire, Ancient of Days, and Bridegroom. And while all of these words serve to give us an accurate depiction of the God of the universe, in the midst of all of the metaphors Jesus could have emphasized to describe God, Jesus gives us a profoundly simple way of relating to God—as a parent, as Abba or Father. Can you imagine Jesus's listeners hearing him address God so intimately? Jesus could have prioritized any number of metaphors to relate to God, and yet, he chose Abba, Father.

Jesus was totally Abba-centered. In John 5:19, he says, "Very truly I tell you, the Son can do nothing by himself; he can do only what he sees his Father doing, because whatever the Father does the Son also does." In John 4:34, it says, "'My food,' said Jesus, 'is to do the will of him who sent me and to finish his work.'" Jesus prayed in the garden of Gethsemane during one of the most emotionally difficult times of his life. Mark 14:36 says, "'*Abba*, Father,' he said, 'everything is possible for you. Take this cup from me. Yet not what I will, but what you will.'" If being Christlike is a Christian's priority, and if Christ related to

God mainly as his Son, then perhaps we should learn something valuable from his relationship with and image of God.

The Prodigal Father

Back to the question of how God would relate to you in the midst of your grief. I think God would demonstrate his love toward you the same way a father did to a young man Jesus spoke about in the parable of the prodigal son, or as I like to call it, the parable of the prodigal father (Luke 15:11–32). *Prodigal* can be defined as "rashly wasteful or extravagant."[5] The son was certainly prodigal in his *wild living*, but the father was prodigal in his *wild loving*. Granted, you might not have sinned like the prodigal son, so it might not be a homecoming moment for you. Nonetheless, the parable uses a father figure to symbolize God, giving us some striking insights into God the Father's wildly loving and compassionate nature.

In this parable, Jesus gives us his internal image of God as a powerful, compassionate, and loving Father who embodied the best of both masculine and feminine traits. Yes, the father in the parable is a strong, wealthy, authoritative male, and yet, I think Jesus's image of the Father defies the norms of what many in our society—or in Jesus's own society—consider masculine.

The father in the prodigal story is a dad who obsesses over his son and who is constantly longing and looking for him. He is a dad who hugs and kisses his child. Instead of giving his son a history lesson on what he has done wrong or scolding him in public, which would invariably have pushed the son further down into a pit of shame and despair, the father reminds him of his true identity. The father gives him royal garb and proclaims boldly, "For this *son* of mine" (v. 24, emphasis mine). And the father knows intuitively that his son needs a coat, slippers, and a ring. I know it is stereotypical, but from my perspective, the father, in part, seems like a modern-day, annoyingly loving and compassionate Jewish mother.

I am not suggesting that everyone should start calling God "Mommy." The primary metaphor Jesus gives us for God is that of a father. I am saying that God is at least motherly—a motherly Father. Premier New Testament scholar and historian John Dominic Crossan writes, "Despite its male-oriented prejudice, the biblical term 'father' is often simply a shorthand term for 'father and mother.'"[6] And that makes sense. Genesis 1:27 says, "So God created humankind in his image, in the image of God he created them; male and female he created them" (NRSV). In other words, male and female together demonstrate a complete picture of the image of God.

God desires to be *otherworldly extravagant* (prodigal) toward you, when you grieve, feel beaten up, and hurt deeply. God wants to run passionately toward you; throw his big, strong, gentle arms around you; and kiss you with compassion and tenderness. Not only that, but God longs to clothe you with the finest of robes, place decked-out shoes on your feet, and slide the most beautiful ring on your finger. God longs to do all of this to remind you that no matter who else wanted or didn't want you, he cherishes and loves you as his child. As 1 John 3:1 proclaims, "See what great love the Father has lavished on us, that we should be called children of God!"

The Spirit of God wants to perform spiritual LASIK surgery on you so you can see afresh that he wants to be the perfect, complete parent to you. As you embrace a clearer picture of who God is, you will have a greater desire to spend more time with him in prayer.

The Dog Lover

Let's look at the concept of soul wear from a different perspective. Imagine you are a kindhearted dog lover. You love to pet them. You love to feed and take care of them. You even give money to local dog shelters.

As you are walking down the road eating your leftover sandwich, you see a dog on the side of the road. It looks dirty, hungry, and even a little hurt. You get the sense that the dog might have been abused.

Your heart melts, and you cautiously try to approach it. You want to pet it and offer it some comfort, or at the very least, give it some of the food you were eating. And as you begin to go near it, the dog lowers his mangy head and shrinks back in fear, trying to distance itself from you. You begin to approach it again, and this time it struggles to get behind some brush, away from your gaze and presence.

How sad is that? The dog is deeply afraid of you and wants nothing to do with you—and it has never even met you. It wants nothing to do with you, not because of who you are but because of experiences it has had with other people. If only it knew how loving, kind, and compassionate you really are, it would quickly limp into your arms and experience the joy of being held, fed, and loved back to health.

I think the dog's sad and fearful experience is similar to the way some people view God. There are countless broken, wounded, and hungry people who do not run into the loving arms of God because of a false perception of who he is. Instead of basing their perceptions on the revelation of his character as shown in the parable of the prodigal Father or in the compassionate life of Jesus, people base their perception of God primarily on past experiences. These are typically painful and traumatic experiences they have had with other people, especially early relationships with their own father or mother, or lack thereof.

Such misperceptions must cause God great sadness. If grieving people only knew how loving, kind, and compassionate God really was, they would limp into his arms and experience, perhaps for the very first time, what pure, compassionate, and healing love truly feels like.

God is not mad at you or seeking to pulverize you with a baseball bat. God is not counting the days until you pass away, hoping you will be sizzling in hell like a juicy rib eye for all eternity. God loves you more than you or I will ever know.

I am convinced that the more our internalized image of God is in line with who he really is, the more our prayer lives will become vibrant and consistent.

God Wants to Parent You

I have counseled many brokenhearted people struggling in their prayer lives because of an incorrect image of who God is. God is not an emotionless, ubermasculine, authoritarian military-style God or a busy absentee landlord. God doesn't want to harm you, condemn you, snub you, or ridicule you. God wants to lovingly parent you through this difficult time. He wants to be the most amazing Father, as well as the most amazing Mother, to you during your season of heartbreak so you can be comforted, grow, and grieve well.

I understand if you are angry with God and don't want much to do with him right now. Sometimes, the nature of pain and extreme hurt keeps us balled up, not wanting to open up and risk vulnerability. I am thankful, though, that no matter how you feel, God's loving and graceful grip on you is a whole lot tighter than your grip on him.

I picture God saying to you what Jesus said to the people of the holy city of Jerusalem who felt lost and confused in the midst of calamity and chaos, and who were therefore keeping God at a distance. In Matthew 23:37, Jesus says, "How often I have longed to gather your children together, as a hen gathers her chicks under her wings, but you were not willing." There goes God, being motherly again, a merciful mother hen to be exact, wanting and longing to protect, comfort, guide, and parent his people.

Speaking of mercy, did you know that *mercy* in the Hebrew Bible many times comes from the Hebrew word meaning "womb"?

The psalmist had this meaning in mind when he cried out in Psalm 40:11, "Do not withhold your mercy from me, LORD; may your love and faithfulness always protect me."

Just a few more verses, and we will be finished with your spiritual LASIK surgery. Psalm 103:13–14 says, "As a father has compassion on his children, so the LORD has compassion on those who fear him; for he knows how we are formed, he remembers that we are dust." God understands your frail and wounded heart, and he wants to hold your hand through this painful process, not harm you. "'For I know the plans I have for you,' declares the LORD, 'plans to prosper you and not to harm you, plans to give you hope and a future'" (Jer. 29:11).

The vertical pathway with God is one of the most important relationships you need to get you through your season of heartbreak. God knows you feel broken—as if you can barely make it through another day. He is not about to snuff you out. On the contrary, he knows you might be barely holding on, trying to make sense of your breakup and the chaotic and painful situation you are in. God wants to show you who he really is. God wants to reinvigorate your relationship with him, parent you compassionately, and restore you.

CHAPTER 7

The First Horizontal Pathway
(Connection with Others)

Piglet sidled up to Pooh from behind. "Pooh?"
he whispered.
　　"Yes, Piglet?"
　　"Nothing," said Piglet, taking Pooh's hand.
"I just wanted to be sure of you."
　　　　—A. A. MILNE, *Winnie-the-Pooh*

Years ago, when I was grieving the loss of my relationship with my girlfriend, I attended a lively church service. While singing a worship song that was all about needing God, and God alone, I found myself needing to stop midchorus. Surprised at what was happening, I began to tear up. I realized I could no longer sing the lyrics with authenticity. I began to feel overwhelmed with heavy guilt and shame. I bowed my head and uttered something to myself I never expected to say: "God is not all I need."

Even though I was praying, fasting, reading the Bible, and submitting myself to God, I still hungered for something more—a real-life, flesh-and-blood human being or two who could compassionately enter my incessant loneliness and pain with me. I needed wit(h)nesses, people who made time to be compassionately present and wholeheartedly *with* me; not afraid to enter my dark experiences; and *witness* my sorrow and pain.

Of course, we need God, but God is not all we need. We have God-designed aches and hungers that God alone cannot fill, one of which is human connection. Even monks, priests, and nuns do life together; they are not off in a cave somewhere like a bunch of self-sufficient hermits.

In this chapter we will be looking at connecting with others (the first horizontal pathway) as a necessary God-given means of allowing you to grieve, heal your heartbreak, and move forward with your life.

Just like Frodo needed Samwise and Gandalf, Batman needed Robin, and the apostle Paul needed Barnabas and Mark, you are also going to need journeying partners as you proceed through some of your most painful and lonely times.

The Power of Relationships

Relationships are the entire thrust of the Christian faith. The Old and New Testaments are crammed with evidence that relationships are the very reason for our existence. God, who is a relational Trinity, exists in a threefold state of connection, equality, and love, and he wanted to extend that blessedness to humans. Not only that, God experiences profound parental pleasure when seeing us relate intimately and lovingly with each other. God loves it when we are like him.

While, ironically, our deepest pain comes from wounds inflicted by other people, other people also provide the most healing and growth. While God heals us directly through his Spirit (the vertical pathway), he also heals us indirectly through the wit(h)ness of other people (the first horizontal pathway).

James 5:16 (AMP) says, "Therefore, confess your sins to one another [your false steps, your offenses], and pray for one another, that you may be healed *and* restored. The heartfelt *and* persistent prayer of a righteous man (believer) can accomplish much [when put into action and made effective by God—it is dynamic and can have tremendous power]."

Prioritizing the vertical relationship with God is vital, but you will also need to find a caring and praying community in which you can be gut-wrenchingly open and honest about your breakup and grief process. Author and spiritual director Beth Allen Slevcove discusses her own desperate need for community during seasons of grief:

> Grief, as we know, often feels like being held under water. Sometimes what we need is to buddy breathe. Buddy breathing happens when a scuba diver loses his or her air supply and another diver comes alongside and shares air, allowing both to breathe until they surface. I've done a lot of buddy breathing through my journeys of grief.[1]

Finding healing in community is not an alternative or fallback plan for those who do not have enough faith in God. It is a biblical imperative and part of God's gold standard for successful healing and living life to its fullest. Finding people to share your story with and experiencing their authentic, loving wit(h)ness as a result will allow you to grieve well.

There is plenty of research confirming the truth of Scripture regarding the power of relationships. A research study of nine thousand people found that close friendships and marriage afforded people approximately one decade of life.[2] Another study of more than three hundred thousand people who were followed for seven and a half years showed they had a 50 percent greater chance of surviving and thriving than those who did not have close relationships.[3] Loving relationships are like super vitamins with potent probiotics in that they nurture us and prolong our days.

God knows what he is doing. He gave us "the greatest commandment" for a reason. God is not a cosmic killjoy who wants to rob us of life by asking us to obey stuffy, outdated commandments. He gave us timeless—forever-contemporary—truths and wisdom so we can experience a truly abundant life. Loving relationships with God and others are key to spiritual and emotional survival, and if we need them in the good times, imagine how much more we are going to need them during the times we are feeling stuck and hopeless, holding shattered hearts in our hands.

Another way to understand the power of connection is to examine what happens when there is a lack of it. Let's talk briefly about loneliness.

Loneliness Kills

One of life's greatest tragedies is that after a breakup people grieve alone. We don't flourish when we're lonely. Social researcher James House says, "The magnitude of risk associated with disconnection and social isolation is comparable with that of cigarette smoking."[4] John Cacioppo, one of the leading researchers in the world on loneliness, says that loneliness increases suicide, lowers a person's immune system, and decreases the quality of sleep. It is also associated with an increased negative view of oneself and others.[5] Feeling alone and isolated has devastating consequences. We are not meant to journey alone.

Vanessa's Story

Vanessa, a Christian plagued by guilt and shame, came for therapy after her breakup with her boyfriend James. She believed sex before marriage was wrong, but she thought she would be with James forever, so she gave him her heart and body. Now that he had broken up with her, she was devastated. She thought God was punishing her for her sexual sins. And she couldn't help but think there was something wrong with her. James didn't give her a reason for the breakup. He said only that he loved her but wasn't "in love" with her and had made a decision to end the relationship.

Vanessa loved God but found it increasingly difficult to pray. She was part of a women's small group at church and decided to risk opening up to them. She burst into tears as she told the group how horrible she felt. She told them she no longer felt like a Christian, and with her head down, shared how distant she felt from God. She told them about her and James's sins, and then she sat there and cried. Feeling deep compassion for Vanessa, the five women in the group held her, prayed for her, and comforted her. And Vanessa's story led to sharing the truth about lingering pain and shame felt by others in the group. They, too, felt distant from God—the sting of sin. There was not a dry eye in the group.

It was a transformative moment for everyone, especially Vanessa. She took a daring risk to open up in a way that she never had before and felt her aloneness dissipate. It brought tremendous healing for her. The next day she found she was able to pray for the first time in a long time. Eventually, she also noticed that the more connected she felt with God and others, the less she criticized, shamed, and blamed herself.

God allowed her to see in a deeply experiential way that the power of connection and community was not only important but vital to her being alive in Christ. God reminded her daily as she read 1 Corinthians 12 that participating as a member of the body of Christ was essential to her growth and development as a believer.

The eye cannot say to the hand, "I don't need you!" And the head cannot say to the feet, "I don't need you!" . . . God has put the body together, giving greater honor to the parts that lacked it, so that there should be no division in the body, but that its parts should have equal concern for each other. If one part suffers, every part suffers with it; if one part is honored, every part rejoices with it.

Now you are the body of Christ, and each one of you is a part of it. (vv. 21, 24–27)

Vanessa became a champion of all things community. Two years later, she felt a tremendous call to reach out to other struggling women and became a committed and anointed small group leader. She has made a tremendous and lasting impact in her community and sees relationships with God and others as inseparable.

We Need Relationships

We will always walk with a limp if we fail to embrace the cross paradigm of healing, wholeness, and vitality. In other words, we will miss out on vital relational pathways that are needed to grieve well, grow well, and live an expansive and epic life. We need the vertical pathway (connection with God) and the first horizontal pathway (connection with others) from womb to tomb, from the cradle to the grave.[6] That is how God created us. Relationships with others need to be paramount in your season of heartbreak and for the rest of your life.

Now let's look at another vital relationship—the second horizontal pathway, cultivating a relationship with yourself.

CHAPTER 8

The Second Horizontal Pathway
(Connection with Yourself)

Do not seek revenge or bear a grudge
against anyone among your people,
but love your neighbor as yourself.
—LEVITICUS 19:18

Jim was a huge, intimidating military guy I met at church. One day he asked to meet for lunch to talk about some things that were bothering him. During lunch, he talked about how he was desperately "trying to be a Christian" after his recent breakup with his fiancée. With his head down and his shoulders slumped, he told me he was struggling with smoking, pornography, and "cursing up a storm." He said that while some weeks he was able to break free from the addictions, others he was not. He couldn't understand why he was struggling so much. He appeared to be filled with shame, and he was being really hard on himself.

I slowly pushed my chair toward him, looked him straight in his saddened eyes, and asked him a simple question. "Jim, do you love yourself?"

"Huh?" he said.

"Do you love yourself?"

For a split second, I thought he was going to give me a karate chop to the throat. I was grateful that didn't happen, but I became nervous about his conservative Christian background and thought he might see me as a heretic for asking him that question.

But he lowered his voice and said, "Mark, no one has ever asked me that question before." This was a thirty-five-year-old guy who was raised as a Christian and who had been in churches his entire life, and no one had ever asked him whether he was following the latter part of the second greatest commandment, "Love your neighbor *as yourself*" (emphasis mine). After I asked him the oddly provocative question, we had a deep conversation about him loving himself and how that would look practically in the midst of his brokenness. As a result of our discussion, he came to a profound realization that he didn't have to hate, judge, or condemn himself in the midst of his current struggles (which he confessed he was doing plenty of). He later told me that was a pivotal shift in his grieving journey.

Love Thyself

You need to love yourself. Does that sound weird? Does that sound heretical? Like New Age sewage? Are we allowed to love ourselves, as Christians? Isn't it sinful or selfish? Don't we love ourselves too much already, especially if we live in the spoiled, hyper-pleasure-focused Western society?

First, it is not sinful and selfish to love ourselves. It is sinful and selfish if we elevate our love for ourselves over and above God and others, which is another word for pride and narcissism. Second, I don't think we love ourselves as much as we think we do. America's daily consumption of drugs and alcohol and dreadful diet of processed sugars while obsessively binge-watching oxymoronic fake/reality TV shows is not loving ourselves. Engaging in such activities can actually be harmful, and in some instances hateful toward ourselves.

Unfortunately, in my work as a pastor and a therapist, I find Christians to be some of the most self-deprecating people I have ever met. Not only do many of us not love ourselves, we do not even like ourselves. This is probably because of a lack of solid teaching on the subject or an overemphasis on "the depravity of man" types of doctrines. When was the last time you heard a sermon called "The Three Biblical Steps to Loving Yourself"? My guess is you have never heard anything even remotely close. This lack of self-love saddens me tremendously, and I am sure it grieves the heart of God that we ignore the second part of the greatest commandment in Mark 12:31, to "love your neighbor as yourself." And that is to our detriment. If anyone should be connoisseurs of a holistic love, it should be Christians whose God *is* love.

Artery Clogs

One of the biggest obstacles to Jim's and others' ability to overcome sin and walk in freedom and intimacy with Jesus is unhealthy shame. Curt Thompson, a Christian psychiatrist, well-known speaker, and author of *The Soul of Shame: Retelling the Stories We Believe About Ourselves*, writes, "Shame is not just a consequence of something our first parents did in the Garden of Eden. It is the emotional weapon that evil uses to (1) corrupt our relationships with God and each other, and (2) disintegrate any and all gifts of vocational vision and creativity."[1]

When thinking about unhealthy shame, I am reminded of clogged up fuel injectors. In cars, fuel injectors are tiny valves that open and close in response to electrical signals from the car's computer. They open, and release fuel to the engine. Sometimes, though, grime and dirt build up in the valves, which causes the car not to accelerate or even start. Shame, condemnation, and harshness toward yourself can clog your spiritual and emotional arteries. They can block the divine fuel of freedom and joy from running smoothly through your heart, keeping you bound and joyless, unable to grieve well. They have no place in your life and are contrary to Jesus's redemptive work on your behalf. You have permission to love yourself boldly, deeply, and compassionately.

Love Yourself as God Loves You

Jerry and Denise Basel are codirectors of The Father's Heart, a global care and intensive Christian counseling ministry. One of their main goals and God-inspired missions is to encourage people to love themselves, a practice they dub "the missing commandment." Denise writes, "I have walked many people over to a large mirror outside my office, had them look themselves straight in the eyes, and then encouraged them to verbalize a love for themselves that agrees with God's own deep love for them. This prayer of declaring our love for ourselves is one of the hardest and most powerful prayers we can pray to break lies and strongholds and to free our hearts to love."[2]

Jerry and Denise, and ministers from all over the United States, are seeing the enormous gap within Christian teaching regarding the need to be kind and loving toward oneself. Their goal, and the goal of others who are championing a biblically based understanding of self-compassion, is not to love ourselves as an end in itself, but to treat ourselves the way God would treat us so we may break strongholds and be freer to love God and unchained to wildly love and serve the world.

Tania Bright, the Christian author of *Don't Beat Yourself Up: Learning the Wisdom of Kindsight*, writes about the power of self-compassion. She says, "With true kindsight, instead of beating ourselves up, or—worse still—judging others, the greatest gift we can give is compassion. Compassion will have a far greater chance of combating a negative coping mechanism than condemnation ever will."[3] Self-compassion, one of the missing gems that is birthed from the heart of God, is finally making its way to the church's consciousness.

You might be in one of the most difficult times of your life. You may wish you had done things a lot differently, and now you're beating yourself up. You could be in an addictive loop—coping with your loss in destructive ways to forget about your pain, feeling intense shame, engaging in more destructive activities to cover up the shame, and then feeling more shame in return. Round and round you go. You can either relate to yourself as the Father of love (1 John 4:16) relates to you, or as the father of lies (John 8:44) does. Of course, the better choice is the former.

Kim Fredrickson, the author of *Give Yourself a Break: Turning Your Inner Critic into a Compassionate Friend*, writes, "We are to model ourselves after God in the way he relates to us. His way is to be drawn to vulnerability and struggle, to respond with compassion and guidance, and to also correct whatever sins or mistakes we've made with grace and truth."[4] Imitate the relational style of the Father of love, exterminate the relational style of the father of lies. During your grieving process, you're either treating yourself with compassion or condemnation, with relenting hope or a negative nope, with tender forgiveness or toxic bitterness.

Self-Compassion

I want to briefly mention some incredible research on self-compassion, which suggests an ideal and practical way to relate to and love yourself. Kristin Neff, one of the world's leading self-compassion researchers and authors, has shown that self-compassion increases healthy relationships, motivation, forgiveness, happiness, hopefulness, positivity, wisdom, curiosity, engagement in new experiences, agreeableness, extroversion, and conscientiousness, while also decreasing shame and depression.[5] Wow. That is some good stuff.

Neff defines self-compassion as the relationship among three main components experienced in the midst of suffering or personal failure: self-kindness, common humanity, and mindfulness. Self-kindness involves treating yourself as you would treat a loving friend in the midst of his or her pain and suffering—with kindness, warmth, and genuine care, rather than attacks, harshness, judgment, and criticism. Instead of engaging in self-hatred, self-kindness allows people to treat themselves gently and compassionately despite their flaws and foibles.

Common humanity is central to self-compassion and recognizes that all human beings are flawed, fractured, wounded, broken, and prone to making mistakes. Keeping common humanity in mind during personal failure provides an invitation to bring compassion into one's experience. The opposite of common humanity is the tendency to isolate oneself when in distress. Isolation tends to breed self-judgment and feelings of disconnection from other human beings.

Mindfulness, the last component of self-compassion, is being aware of one's experience in the present moment with acceptance. Engaging in mindfulness allows a person to experience thoughts and feelings as separate entities. In other words, thoughts are not you, it is you who are having thoughts. Mindfulness allows people to keep a balanced view of negative emotions and experiences while cultivating an open and flexible perspective. The opposite of mindfulness is overidentification, where people identify and fuse with negative thoughts and feelings.

For example, in the aftermath of a breakup, it's easy to have thoughts such as: *I am just not good enough* or *I am trash* or *No one will ever date me again.* The problem is that people fuse with those thoughts and believe them to be true. The alternative is to be *mindful*, or *aware* of them, while they occur. *I am just not good enough* becomes *Oh, I am having the thought that I am just not good enough*. Mindfulness creates space around thoughts so people can choose to believe them or not.

Self-Compassion and the Bible

Even though self-compassion is rarely emphasized in Christian circles, all of Neff's components of self-compassion can be found in the Bible. For example, her first component, self-kindness, is a clear biblical principle and is neither narcissistic nor evil. As discussed already, in the midst of our suffering we can either relate to ourselves as the Father of love does or as the father of lies does. If we want to be like God whose nature is to be comforting and compassionate toward us when we are suffering, then we should be comforting and compassionate toward ourselves as well.

The second component, common humanity, is also a principle found in the Bible. It is an acknowledgment that "no test or temptation that comes your way is beyond the course of what others have had to face" (1 Cor. 10:13 MSG). Common humanity also reminds us that "all have sinned and fall short of the glory of God" (Rom. 3:23). Henri Nouwen, a spiritual mentor, author, and teacher to many in various Christian traditions, writes about the importance of acknowledging our common humanity. "The way we let go of our losses and sorrows is by connecting our personal pain to the great suffering of humanity, by understanding our own grief and loss as part of the larger picture of the world. For we are not the only ones who suffer in the world. Nor are we all alone."[6]

We are never alone when we suffer. We have a cloud of faithful witnesses from the past and present who have suffered as we do and whose tears join ours in the pond of human suffering. We are all affected by our own sin and, tragically, by the sin of others. We are all flawed and wounded, and, as a result, we have all experienced loss and suffering.

Lastly is Neff's component of *mindfulness*. Don't be weirded out by the term. It is not a spooky word that we should be afraid of because the Bible does, in fact, call us to be mindful. Psalm 4:4 says, "Tremble and do not sin; when you are on your beds, search your hearts and be silent." Colossians 4:2 says, "Devote yourselves to prayer, being watchful and thankful." Mindfulness, searching our hearts, being watchful, tuning in, and centering all mean pretty much the same thing: awareness. The Bible calls us to live wide-eyed and openhearted with unblocked ears and an uncluttered heart. As ambassadors of Christ, we are always encouraged to be aware of how we engage God, ourselves, and the world around us.

Secular mindfulness encourages moment-to-moment awareness of thoughts. In other words, when thoughts come the task is just to notice them floating by as if on a leaf floating down a river. The Bible calls us not only to be mindfully aware but also to "take captive every thought to make it obedient to Christ" (2 Cor. 10:5), which is one of the main differences between the two. As Christians, we are to notice the thoughts as they arise *and* surrender the lies in our minds to Christ so that he will replace them with truth.

It is vital that we include God in the mindfulness practice because our awareness antennas are a bit rickety due to the fall. We need God to guide us and convict us when we embrace lies. God's conviction allows us to distinguish between the truth and lies. But what does it mean to say that God convicts us?

Contrary to what many people think, the word *convict* doesn't have anything to do with making people feel really bad. Coming from the Greek word *elegcho*, *convict* means "to expose, reveal, or bring to light." A Christian approach to mindfulness relies on the Holy Spirit to reveal and bring to light what is really going on in one's heart and life. That is why Ephesians 5:13 says, "But everything exposed [*elegcho*] by the light becomes visible—and everything that is illuminated becomes a light." In order to experience truth-based awareness, we need the light of God's Spirit to expose what is hidden in the dark recesses of our hearts. As Christians, we don't merely *let go*, as in the case of mindfulness; rather, we are called to *let God*.

Example of Biblical Self-Compassion

Sarah came to see me for counseling after she'd broken up with her boyfriend three months earlier. Even though she intended to grieve well, her Montu-like experience sometimes threw her into bouts of depression. She had been connecting with God in prayer, especially when taking long walks through the park near her home. She had several friends who know about her breakup, and they checked in with her weekly. And in our counseling sessions we had been working through her grief, shame, and self-criticism through contemplative prayer and self-compassion.

One day when she was alone, she noticed her anxiety level was high and caught herself having a lot of negative thoughts toward herself and her ex. She wrote them in her journal and shared some of them with me:

> This is too hard. Why do I have to go through this when everyone else is happy and in a relationship?
>
> I don't like how I look today. I look freakin' ugly!
>
> I hate my ex. Why did he do this to me?
>
> I wish he would be as hurt as I am right now. I hate this. How can I call myself a Christian and wish someone else harm?

When she finally realized her thoughts and emotions were starting to snowball, she practiced self-compassion. First, she sat down and became mindful, or aware, of her thoughts and experiences without judging herself. With her train of negative thoughts running wild, she felt anxiety in her stomach and sadness weighing her down. In that moment of distress, she reminded herself that she was not alone in her pain and that many people, even Christians who love God, struggle with negative thoughts and emotional pain (common humanity).

Sarah read Philippians 4:8 to herself, "Whatever is true, whatever is noble, whatever is right, whatever is pure, whatever is lovely, whatever is admirable—if anything is excellent or praiseworthy—think about such things." She placed her warm hand over her heart and offered herself compassion. She spoke cherished Bible truths over herself out loud: "You are a beloved daughter of God. You are forgiven and loved. Your sadness is normal and is a sign that you loved deeply. You will get through this." After her self-compassion exercise, she felt God's peace and continued on with the rest of her day.

Self-compassion is a sacred relational attitude and virtue. Christians should prioritize self-compassion in discipleship for optimum relational health.

Compassionate Self-Talk

Another practical way you can love yourself is to speak to yourself the way God would speak to you. The apostle Paul writes, "Do not let any unwholesome talk come out of your mouths, but only what is helpful for building others up according to their needs, that it may benefit those who listen" (Eph. 4:29). While the verse refers specifically to how we are to speak to one another, it makes sense to apply the concept when speaking to ourselves as well.

For example, it is easy to be hard on yourself during your season of heartbreak. You might speak to yourself the way the father of lies speaks to you, by criticizing your emotional condition, judging how you look, bashing yourself for your lack of spiritual vitality—and the list goes on. The apostle Paul encourages us to not let "unwholesome" talk come out of our mouths. That word *unwholesome* comes from a Greek word that can mean "rotten or bad." In other words, stop trash-talking yourself. Say things to yourself that are encouraging and that are going to build you up, not tear you down. If you can't picture a loving and compassionate God saying the negative comment to you, or if it isn't something you would say to your dearest friend, then it is probably not something you should say to yourself.

Whenever we think about the fruit of the Spirit, we usually think of demonstrating the fruit of the Spirit toward others. How powerful would it be to pray for more love, joy, peace, forbearance, kindness, goodness, faithfulness, gentleness, and self-control toward yourself during your time of grief (Gal. 5:22–23)? I can assure you, relating to yourself the way God relates to you is a life-changing experience.

They Are All Connected

Loving yourself via self-compassion is not an end in itself and should not be isolated from loving God and loving your neighbor. The Lorraine cross paradigm of connection, healing, and transformation is symbolized by one cross with different pathways, each interdependent and connected with one another.

For example, a recent study demonstrates beautifully the interconnectedness between self-compassion, relationship with others, and emotional health after a traumatic event. In regard to emotional health, the study specifically looked at post-traumatic stress disorder (PTSD), generalized anxiety disorder (GAD), and depression. The researchers studied a pool of individuals who had recently experienced a potentially traumatic event. They measured their degree of social support and self-compassion through the use of various evidence-based self-reported assessments. The study found that those who had a greater degree of social support, via family, friends, and significant others, also had a greater degree of self-compassion and a decrease in symptoms of PTSD, GAD, and depression. The researchers believed that self-compassion and relationships were interrelated. They concluded that "social support may reduce symptoms of PTSD, GAD, and depression through increased self-compassion in those who experienced a trauma."[7] Love from others increases our ability to love ourselves.

God's love is also essential for being able to love ourselves and love others. You might have heard the expression, "You can't love others until you love yourself." I don't think you can truly love yourself until you first allow yourself to be loved by God. As 1 John 4:19 reminds us, "We love because he first loved us."

As we experience love from others, including God, we internalize the love and that increases our experience of feeling lovable and our capacity to love ourselves. The more we love ourselves, the less shame we have, which frees us to love others and reach out to God. Loving God, loving others, and loving ourselves are all connected. They cannot be separated and are indispensable for your season of heartbreak or your lifelong journey.

Grieving Practices

Rarely does reading information result in transformation. That is why the Bible uses action words and phrases such as "do likewise" (Luke 10:37), "go and make" (Matt. 28:19), "put on" (Eph. 6:11; Col. 3:10), "put it into practice" (Phil. 4:9), "reflect" (2 Tim. 2:7), "meditate" and "consider" (Ps. 119:15), "follow" (Luke 9:23), and "clothe yourselves" (Col. 3:12; 1 Peter 5:5).

We journeyed through the process of grief in part I, and looked at relational pathways that are integral to healing your heartbreak in part II. In this section, part III, we will look at specific, heavenly down-to-earth practices you can engage in that will allow the "Sonlight" and the wind of God's grace to come through the window of your soul in a deeper measure.

Throughout history people have engaged in most

of the mental and physical spiritual practices we will examine. Some of these will be like life preservers for you and some you may decide to throw aside. You may already be enjoying certain practices that are not included in these chapters, and that's okay. The point is to find exercises that work for you and practice them daily, weekly, or monthly.

As you engage in these practices, notice how each helps you connect more fully to one or all three of the relational pathways discussed in the previous section. The exercises herein have changed my life and helped me grieve well, and I hope they do the same for you.

CHAPTER 9

Prayer

*The Word lies hidden in the soul, unnoticed and unheard
unless room is made for it in the ground of hearing, otherwise it is not heard; but all voices and all sounds must cease
and perfect stillness must reign there, a still silence.*

—Meister Eckhart

There are dozens of ways and places to pray. You can pray
prayers of thanksgiving, intercession, consecration, exal-
tation, lament, and request. You can also pray angry prayers
(protest), prayers (praying for a million things at once), bullet
prayers (very focused and specific), and the list goes on. You can
pray in the wilderness, in the bathroom, on the beach, at work,
or really anywhere you want because God is everywhere.

In this chapter, I want to talk about a few uncommon but
wonderful prayer practices that can help you connect to the vertical pathway (relationship with God), namely centering prayer,
weeping and crying out, and imaginative meditative prayer. I use
the word *uncommon* because Christians may or may not engage
in these types of prayers very often, although some engage in a
few of them without even knowing it. These practices are rooted
firmly in the Scriptures and the Christian tradition. May you
find them helpful for enabling you to grieve well and grow closer

to God, not only during this current season of heartbreak but throughout the rest of your life.

Centering Prayer

Centering prayer can be one of the most difficult prayers to engage in because it requires stillness and silence, which are completely countercultural and counter-ego. Stillness and silence are countercultural to our drive-through, drive-by, and driven society that fosters a jittery nervous system and type A(DHD) personalities. Many people, therefore, think of stillness, silence, and solitude as alien planets too far outside their solar system to explore. Additionally, the notion of sitting still—doing nothing in many people's minds—is not going to skyrocket one's career and win the esteem of a culture that values and honors the doers, the go-getters, and the fast and furious.

Centering prayer is also counter-ego because, when the brightness of God's loving floodlight shines on our wounded souls, it can disrupt what we know and believe to be true about God, ourselves, and the world. And since the ego likes sameness and the status quo, it tends to run away from the brightness of God's floodlight the way little bugs scurry away when someone lifts a rock and exposes them to the sun. The ego is deathly afraid of change because it sends a person into the unknown. Even if the change God invites us into is beautiful, good, and liberating, our self-protective ego tends to prefer what is familiar, even if it is ugly, sinful, and binding.

For the most part, contemplative prayer is meant to be *wordless* yet *full* of the *Word*. Thomas Merton, a well-known Catholic writer, contemplative, and Trappist monk, reminds us of the wordless level of prayer. He writes, "The deepest level of communication is not communication, but communion. It is wordless . . . beyond speech . . . beyond concept."[1] In this type of prayer, words, which are humanly constructed, are not as important as communication coming straight from one's spirit directly to the Holy Spirit. The sacred word that is used in contemplative prayer, which we will explore shortly, is mostly a reminder to be present in this wordless space.

On the other hand, it is a Word-full space. The gospel of John says, "The Word became flesh and made his dwelling among us. . . . full of grace and truth" (John 1:14). Prayer is meant to be communion with the Word, who is Jesus Christ. In contemplative prayer, we are less interested in quoting Scripture or making requests, both of which are perfectly fine in other contexts. We are much more interested in being still in the presence of the Word, allowing ourselves to be captivated by the beloved Christ.

Origins of Centering Prayer

Centering prayer has its origins in the teachings of Jesus. It is a specific type of praying that is based on a verse in the Sermon on the Mount: "When you pray, go into your room, close the door and pray to your Father, who is unseen. Then your Father, who sees what is done in secret, will reward you" (Matt. 6:6). Centering prayer was developed by the Desert Fathers and Mothers, who were devout God-lovers and ascetics who lived in Egypt around the third century AD. Thomas Keating, a contemporary Trappist monk and priest, popularized the approach and formalized the prayer in an understandable and easy-to-follow format.[2]

In a metaphorical sense, Keating postulated that the inner room can be thought of as the deepest place of your heart where you *shut out* every form of distraction and cacophonic sound, while *shutting in* the very presence of God. This inner room is where a mysterious and profound dance takes place between God's Spirit and your spirit, God's heart and your heart. It is a place where the reward, or present, is God's presence.

Centering prayer also has roots in Ephesians 3:14–19:

For this reason I kneel before the Father, from whom every family in heaven and on earth derives its name. I pray that out of his glorious riches he may strengthen you with power through his Spirit in your inner being, so that Christ may dwell in your hearts through faith. And I pray that you, being rooted and established in love, may have power, together with all the Lord's holy people, to grasp how wide and long and high and deep is the love of Christ, and to know this love that surpasses knowledge—that you may be filled to the measure of all the fullness of God.

God wants to meet you in the deep broken places of your heart and strengthen you. In the quiet place produced by centering prayer, God's desire is to increase your faith in the beauty of Christ and to infuse you with his vast love. God wants your inner roots to reach down deep to his presence through centering prayer where they can absorb the necessary nutrients to grow and bear fruit—so you, as well as those with whom you come in contact, can enjoy it. You have lost a person you cared for deeply, but you have an opportunity to gain a fuller measure of a loving, intimate relationship with God.

Centering Prayer in a Nutshell

Keating recommends practicing centering prayer twice a day for about twenty minutes.[3] It is common for some people to engage in centering prayer when they get up in the morning and before they go to bed. Some, including me, use a timer with a soft bell to signal the end of the twenty minutes. And yes, there is an app for that.

Here's what the practice looks like:

1. Choose a sacred word as a symbol of your intention to consent to God's presence and action within. This could

be any word. I personally have used *Jesus, Abba, Love, Peace,* and others. You can ask the Holy Spirit to speak to your heart, or you can search the Scriptures to find a word that resonates with you. Throughout the centering prayer, whichever word you choose will serve to anchor you to your intention when thoughts distract you. When you are thinking about how miserable you feel or how much your ex is pond scum, for example, your sacred word will gently refocus your mind on being in the presence of God.

2. Sitting comfortably and with your eyes closed, settle yourself, and silently introduce the sacred word as the symbol of your consent to God's presence and action within. Make sure you are in a comfortable position and have all your electronic devices turned off. Unless you're using an app, it is preferable to set your devices out of the room to avoid unnecessary distractions. Be relaxed, but not so much that you could easily fall asleep (though if you do, you probably needed to). Close your eyes and say the sacred word to yourself.

3. When engaged with other thoughts, return ever so gently to the sacred word. The word *thoughts*, here, is all-encompassing. It includes feelings, images, bodily experiences, memories, smells, and brilliant new revelations you think you are receiving. Don't judge yourself if they arise; gently bring your attention to your sacred word and let go of the thoughts, allowing yourself to come back to God's presence. Picture your thoughts as if they are on clouds that are floating away, or on lily pads floating downstream. You might get lost in thoughts a dozen times, but gently bring yourself back to God's presence.

4. At the end of the prayer period, remain in silence with eyes closed for a couple of minutes. The last guideline is to transition back into your routines peacefully and with reverence. It is an acknowledgment that you have just

experienced a special moment with God. Feel free to end this time with one of your favorite verses or the Lord's Prayer.

It Takes Practice

Most people avoid such intimacy and vulnerability with God for a reason. Keating writes, "Thoughts are integral, inevitable, and a normal part of centering prayer. They contribute to the unloading of our childhood wounds and help clear the emotional debris of a lifetime."[4] You may encounter a lot of emotional stuff when you engage God in this way, such as repressed memories, painful sensations, anxiety, and uncomfortable emotions. This is normal.

Being still and silent while spending time with God can also be difficult because you might already be experiencing intense emotion and rampant negative thoughts due to your breakup. If you try it a few times but are unable to stay seated for the entire twenty minutes, then go easy on yourself. People who begin a running program with a ten-mile goal in mind may be able to run only half a mile at first. It's the same with centering prayer. Developing your silence and solitude muscles takes practice.

My Own Centering Prayer Journey

When I started learning how to connect with God through centering prayer, it was really difficult. As I sat silently in prayer, focused on the sacred word and enjoying intimacy with God, painful mom-and-dad memories often rose to the surface. Not my idea of fun, especially right after I had experienced a breakup. It was God's way of helping me heal and freeing me from the extra baggage I had been carrying around for many years.

There were also many times I set my intention and began the prayer, and twenty seconds into it a million thoughts raced through my mind, many of which were about my ex. In a matter of seconds I went from saying, "She is a child of God and deeply loved" to "She is the spawn of Satan, and I hope her new boyfriend is a complete jerk."

Sometimes, I was in the God-zone, experiencing the blessedness of solitude, and then moments later I found myself salivating over thoughts of greasy cheeseburgers and a pint of cookies and cream ice cream I had in the freezer.

Initially, sitting still and silent was like climbing Mount Everest in blizzard conditions, wearing worn-out tennis shoes and carrying a one-hundred-pound knapsack. It seemed impossible. With years of practice, I have come to highly value and appreciate that special intimate time with God. Although it can still be hard to sit still, I know that praying is how my heart cries out for home, and it is where God whispers, "Welcome home, my beloved; I missed you."

Thirsty? Then Drink

The psalmist writes, "As the deer pants for streams of water, so my soul pants for you, my God. My soul thirsts for God, for the living God" (Ps. 42:1–2). Is this the cry of your heart? If not, that is okay. Everyone is in a different spiritual space. God loves you where you are. If you have a deeper hunger to connect with God, then take a risk and "taste and see that the LORD is good" (Ps. 34:8). If you have a deeper thirst to experience the love and tenderness of God, then centering prayer can help you encounter the One who said, "Whoever drinks the water I give them will never thirst. Indeed, the water I give them will become in them a spring of water welling up to eternal life" (John 4:14).

Leanne Payne, a contemporary contemplative author and speaker who recently passed away, wrote beautifully concerning prayer. "In God's Presence, we've come before the One who speaks worlds into being, who delights in speaking new worlds of *being* into our very souls, affirming, as He does so, those very parts of ourselves that have (for whatever reason) not been called forth and blessed in our families and earthly relationships."[5]

I am convinced that God's desire is for every person to be able to shout with confidence, "I belong to my beloved, and his desire is for me" (Song 7:10). May you find a deeper place of intimacy with God as you journey, through the practice of centering prayer. May you be strengthened and encouraged. In this difficult season of heartbreak, may you experience the new life-giving words God is whispering into your being, fortifying your identity as his beloved child.

Weeping and Crying Out

Weeping and crying out are two other uncommon practices of prayer that can help you grieve well. You might already be doing them, but I want you to know what these prayer practices look like in detail so that when you experience them, you are able to acknowledge and embrace them as vital modes of connecting with God.

The reason weeping and crying out are considered practices is that it takes practice to become comfortable with experiencing intense emotions and tears and with using your voice to cry out to God. Engaging in weeping and crying out might feel like you are walking on a waterbed rather than solid ground. It feels chaotic and messy, and for some people, sacrilegious, or at the very least, like it is disappointing to God. These practices are seldom talked about and are considered uncommon, but they are extremely important types of prayer, especially in the midst of grief.

Weeping is an act of crying, sobbing, and mourning while typically experiencing tears. Loss and tragedy typically lie beneath weeping, as does deep pain, sadness, and grief.

Crying out is slightly different, although it can go hand in hand with weeping. Crying out is the act of raising your voice in lament, concern, or demand for justice.

Of course, people can weep or cry out because they are happy and filled with joy, but for the most part, when the Bible speaks of weeping or crying out, it's usually in the context of loss, or what Walter Brueggemann, an Old Testament scholar, calls disorientation.[6] He writes, "It constitutes a dismantling of the old, known world and a relinquishment of safe, reliable confidence in God's good creation. The movement of dismantling includes a rush of negativities, including rage, resentment, guilt, shame, isolation, despair, hatred, and hostility."[7]

Let's look at weeping and crying out in more detail.

Weeping

Weeping is a wonderfully intense physical and emotional process, a gift that God has given to us to deal with our various disorientations. It might not feel like a gift when we are experiencing it. I would much rather experience joy than grief. Nonetheless, weeping allows us to enter into our loss in a profound way, and when given to God, weeping becomes deeply hallowed prayers. That's right. Weeping and tears are prayers to God. Although weeping is usually done without words, God understands the messages behind them. The psalmist writes, "Record my misery; list my tears on your scroll—are they not in your record?" (Ps. 56:8). God understands the language of tears. He has a sacred scroll with a record of the details of your tender tears of affliction. God never forgets them.

Chris Ann Waters writes in her book, *Seasons of Goodbye*, about the importance of tears:

> When we have loved someone or something, love is never over, so neither is our sense of loss. The tears of change that flow down our hearts are tears signifying participation in life. Tears reveal our connection to someone or something else. We chose to love. Tears are not a sign of weakness or

embarrassment for men or women. Tears are water, a sign of life, an element necessary for growth. When shared, love changes and brings tears to the eyes, they are but symbols of our involvement in life.[8]

Your tears are not a sign of weakness but a powerful symbol that shows you were courageous; you took a risk on the unpredictable nature of love and loved anyway. Those who have ceased to cry have ceased to love and participate fully in life.

Weeping also has a practical function. Tears are a God-given language we have from birth that communicates distress and loss. Tears are designed to communicate to those most important to us that we need them to come close and offer comfort or sustenance. Science backs this up.

Lucy Biven and Jaak Panksepp, a renowned neurobiologist, believe there are at least seven different emotional systems in the brain that generate distinct emotions and behaviors when activated.[9] When we are grieving, our panic/grief system is activated. Once it is activated, some people yell out in distress or cry. Some move toward others who love them; others move away to soothe themselves. Crying, like other grieving behaviors, is meant to activate in other people the part of the brain Panksepp calls the "CARE system," a system of tending and befriending. When activated, the CARE system moves people around us to offer compassionate care and comfort.

John Bowlby, a famous English psychiatrist, made researching relationships his life's work. He noted that the weeping that takes place when an adult loses a loved one correlates with the weeping that takes place when a child misses an absent parent.[10] The child's tears communicate, "Please, take care of me. Come here. I need you right now." They signal the need for the mother, father, or primary caretaker to return. They cue the parent to give the child food or hugs and cuddles, which make the child feel safe and secure again.

Though you are not crying out for your mother, your tears are an unconscious plea for your ex to come back. They are saying, "I love you. I miss you. I need you. I am in so much pain. Please come back. I want to feel safe and secure in your arms again." I say this with deep compassion. Unfortunately, your ex is probably gone and no amount of tears will bring him or her back. Thankfully, God sees your tears, hears your weeping, and is always drawn to the inner ache of his beloveds.

David spoke about God's soft spot for his weeping children.

I am worn out from my groaning.

All night long I flood my bed with weeping
    and drench my couch with tears.
My eyes grow weak with sorrow;
    they fail because of all my foes.

Away from me, all you who do evil,
    for the LORD has heard my weeping.
The LORD has heard my cry for mercy;
    the LORD accepts my prayer.
All my enemies will be overwhelmed with shame and anguish;
    they will turn back and suddenly be put to shame.

(Ps. 6:6–10)

Have you experienced that kind of grief because of your breakup? Tears that could drench a couch? Crying that leaves your eyes so painful and puffy that you can barely see? David, a warrior and very much a man's man, surely did. He wrote in another psalm, "When my prayers returned to me unanswered, I went about mourning as though for my friend or brother. I bowed my head in grief as though weeping for my mother" (Ps. 35:13–14). He never allowed fear of being thought weak to keep him from expressing himself authentically to God. When David experienced brokenness, he let God know. And God heard his weeping, saw his tears, and accepted them as heartfelt prayer.

Crying Out

Have you recently raised a fist at God in protest? Have you yelled, complained, gotten angry, doubted, or questioned God in your excruciatingly painful season of heartbreak? Such interactions with God are often called prayers of lament.

Maybe breaking up with your ex has been the best thing that ever happened to you and you have instantly moved to prayers of praise and thanksgiving. That is awesome. On the other hand, maybe you have to wail prayers of lament before you get there. That is okay too.

Psalm 88 is an example of a prayer of lament, though it is one of the rare laments that do not end with thanksgiving or praise.

> I am overwhelmed with troubles
>   and my life draws near to death. . . .
> I am confined and cannot escape;
>   my eyes are dim with grief. . . .
> Why, LORD, do you reject me
>   and hide your face from me? . . .
> You have taken from me friend and neighbor—
>   darkness is my closest friend.
>
> (vv. 3, 9, 14, 18)

Can you feel the pain and inner torment? There is such a holy haunting and beautiful darkness that surrounds this psalm. It is such a powerful portrayal of honesty and depth that epitomizes what it means to engage in the uncommon, prayerful practice of crying out to God.

Psalm 88 is a vulnerable and, some would consider, slightly dark worship song written by a passionate God-lover, which pushes up against the "I always have to have it all together" mentality so pervasive in our culture and churches. When was the last time you heard a congregation sing this type of song? I have never heard a song quite like that in a worship service. As a worship leader, if I ended a song with "darkness is my closest friend" in church, I think some of the older folks out of loving concern would immediately start a secret prayer-chain and others might question my salvation.

Sometimes the most faithful thing we can do is that which appears faithless. There are times when singing songs of lament, which appear to hyper-religious folk as faithless, would be far more honest than singing today's all-too-common, upbeat, pop praise songs. Sadly, if there were a church where songs of lament were sung on a continual basis, there might be many who choose to never return to the church, judging the members as unspiritual or worse, unsaved. That judgment couldn't be further from the truth.

Hidden Rules

It is healthy to inquire about any irrational rules or unnecessary culturally formed beliefs you have about emotions so those beliefs do not keep you from grieving well. Some believe, for example, that so-called negative emotions such as anger, frustration, depression, loneliness, and the like are not Christian or godly emotions. Some people believe they are not glorifying God if they're not constantly showing the "joy of the Lord." No matter how they feel inside, they believe they have to wear a Sunday smile because "that is how God wants me to deal with emotions." They believe showing sadness and hurt ruins their witness. Ironically, authenticity is the best witness in this postmodern culture, where everyone is suspicious and weary of the salesperson mentality.

Is crying only for babies—is it a practice we grow out of as we become adults? Do you worry that if you allow yourself to feel something intensely you will get lost in a sea of emotions? Is lamenting before God part of your worship? Is it even allowed in your worship? Are you free to experience the primary, universal emotions of anger, sadness, surprise, shame/disgust, fear, and joy? Do you think some are more godly than others? Continue to reflect on your hidden rules and revise them as necessary.

A Time for Weeping and Mourning

The wisdom writer in Ecclesiastes reminds us that we will all experience different seasons in our lives.

> There is a time for everything,
>   and a season for every activity under the heavens:
>
> a time to be born and a time to die,
> a time to plant and a time to uproot,
> a time to kill and a time to heal,
> a time to tear down and a time to build,
> *a time to weep* and a time to laugh,
> *a time to mourn* and a time to dance.

(Eccl. 3:1–4, emphasis mine)

The word *mourn* comes from a root word meaning "to wail or howl" and has come to mean "to beat the breast or lament."[11] Mourning encompasses what we mean by *crying out*. Both weeping and crying out in despair or protest are important practices we should not easily dismiss from our repertoire of prayers. There is a time for both. While you can't always flick a switch and weep or cry out on the spot, I suggest that when such emotions and impulses do spring up like a fountain you embrace them as precious gifts.

God Hears You

God listens to your screams and cries of pain and shame in this difficult season. Exodus 2:23–24 says, "The Israelites groaned in their slavery and cried out, and their cry for help because of their slavery went up to God. *God heard* their groaning and he remembered his covenant with Abraham, with Isaac and with Jacob" (emphasis mine). And the psalmist confidently declares that God listens, saying, "The righteous cry out, and *the* LORD *hears* them; he delivers them from all their troubles" (Ps. 34:17, emphasis mine).

God is certainly a God who acts, but rest assured that he is also a God who listens, and you can run into his compassionate arms. This is a time, therefore, for you to raise a fist, yell, weep, question, wail, and howl if you need to. Do whatever is honest, whatever is true within your heart. You don't have to fake it. God loves honesty.

It is evident throughout the Bible that God keeps it real with us. So why not keep it real with God? When I read the Bible I often say to myself, "Sheesh, God, do you have to be so honest and say it that way?" When we set our hearts on grieving well, we can be confident that what we "sow with tears" we will eventually "reap with songs of joy" (Ps. 126:5).

Imaginative Meditative Prayer

Another uncommon prayer practice is imaginative meditative prayer. Imaginative prayer takes seriously the command to "Love the Lord your God will all your heart and with all your soul and with all your strength and with all your mind" (Luke 10:27). It is designed to engage all of our senses, including our imagination, in prayer.

I designed a prayer for you to pray during your season of heartbreak, drawing on imaginative prayer of the Ignatian Christian tradition and from loving-kindness meditation. Before I share it with you, however, let me briefly describe the origins of imaginative prayer and give a description of loving-kindness meditation.

Ignatius of Loyola

Ignatius of Loyola was born in 1491 and eventually became an expert in spiritual direction. He believed God could speak to his people through their vivid imaginations and that prayers should be holistic, engaging the mind, heart, and emotions.[12] Ignatius loved immersing himself in the captivating stories of Scripture. He used his imagination to journey into the sacred texts, almost as if he were experiencing a 4-D film. He attempted to live in the story, allowing it to engage all five senses within his imagination.

Although some early Christians opposed the use of the imagination in one's relationship with God, Ignatius did not allow their fears to keep him from using his God-given senses. It appears that as long as his experiences did not contradict God's Word, all was fair in prayer.

Loving-Kindness Meditation

Loving-kindness meditation is a brain-training exercise in which participants repeat loving phrases toward oneself and others as a means to foster an attitude of compassion and goodwill. The loving-kindness exercise fits well within the Christian tradition as we are asked to dwell on "whatever is true, whatever is noble, whatever is right, whatever is pure, whatever is lovely, whatever is admirable" (Phil. 4:8). This has become a secular research-based brain-training exercise as well. The exercise repeated over time actually changes the brain, particularly in the area involved with empathy.[13] Research shows that when practiced over time, the loving-kindness exercise increases compassion, self-compassion, and positive emotions—all while decreasing depression.[14]

The prayer below, "God's Loving-Kindness," combines a loving-kindness meditation with imaginative prayer. Add this formalized prayer to your repertoire and use it when you feel overwhelmed with emotions such as shame, anger, and fear.

Make sure you're seated and comfortable. Become aware of the sacred space and of God's presence. Notice your breath. Feel the air moving into your nostrils and into your body. Breathe in, and breathe out. *Pause for five seconds.*

Take a few moments to attend to your heart. *Pause for five seconds.*

Loving-kindness involves opening and softening the heart. Feel your breath coming and going. Place one or both hands over your heart. Breathe in and out, in and out, thanking God for the breath of life. *Pause for ten seconds.*

This is a sacred space. Allow God to hold you in loving-kindness. As I offer some phrases for you to consider, please feel free to change them to whatever allows you to hold yourself in loving-kindness. If you find yourself distracted by other thoughts or feelings, simply return to your breath, without judgment.

Now imagine yourself enfolded in the arms of a compassionate God. Repeat these phrases to yourself as you breathe in and breathe out:

> May I be held in your loving-kindness.
> May I be well in both body and mind.
> May I continue to grieve well.
> May I learn to forgive and be free.

Pause for ten seconds. Slowly repeat these phrases for five minutes.

Listen to God gently say, "I love holding you in the same way parents love holding their beautiful child. My desire is for you to be well in both body and mind. Do not be afraid, my child, for I will never forsake you. I have come to give you abundant life." *Gently repeat twice.*

Imagine yourself kneeling humbly before Jesus. Imagine his radiance and pleasure in seeing you. Imagine his strength and tenderness. *Pause for ten seconds.*

Imagine yourself putting your pain, shame, anger, and grief in a bowl and presenting them to God. Picture God gently taking the bowl from you.

Listen to God gently say, "You are my beloved child in whom I am well pleased. You are wonderfully and fearfully made. Nothing can separate you from my love. I can see how much pain you are in, and because you hurt, I hurt with you. I will not leave you alone on this healing journey. I love you deeply."

What was that like for you? Were you able to get through the exercise in its entirety? Did you find yourself getting distracted with rambunctious thoughts? Were you able to encounter God and feel a sense of warmth and love? Was your pain too loud to hear anything else?

If it was a positive experience for you, take note and use this meditation when your thoughts seem dismal and your pain feels overwhelming. If it was not a positive experience, that is okay. There is no judgment. You are no less spiritual. Accept yourself for where you are and extend compassion toward yourself and continue to look for spiritual practices that resonate with you.

CHAPTER 10

Holy Huddle

*Anything that's human is mentionable, and anything
that is mentionable can be more manageable.
When we can talk about our feelings, they become
less overwhelming, less upsetting, and less scary.
The people we trust with that important talk can
help us know that we are not alone.*

—MR. FRED ROGERS

After my devastating breakup, I realized I did not have all
the answers. I knew I was bleeding out and needed other
people to come to my aid. It was crucial for me to be around
people experienced in the areas of love, loss, and life. I realized I
could not grieve alone and became desperate to find community.

I quieted the fear-based introvert part of me and told my story
to as many people as I could. I really wanted to learn and grow
from my heartbreak. I sought the wisdom and listening ears of
friends, professors, and even a couple of people I barely knew
(not always the best option). Not everyone had good advice or
even the capacity to listen without making the conversation
about him- or herself, but the experience did help me learn to
distinguish safe and comforting people from oblivious and cold
ones. I started building a network of supportive friends, which

was beneficial not only for my season of heartbreak but for the rest of my life.

There were certain things I could not see because of my pain and confusion, and my holy huddle gave me healthy and fresh perspectives. Proverbs 11:14 says, "In the multitude of counsellors there is safety" (KJV). Find your holy huddle, your people of wisdom and character who can guide you safely through your season of grief. In so doing, you will be putting the first horizontal pathway, the connection we need with others and creation, into practice.

Who Are You Huddling With?

In sports, players regularly form a tight circle to encourage one another and strategize about how to advance against the opponents and win the game. In your holy huddle, a team of like-minded people will listen to your story and encourage you through the struggles that lie ahead. They will help you grieve losses, maintain your balance, and move forward to cross God's goal line. With empathy and compassion, your teammates will help you strategize for success; extinguish harsh judgment, shaming, and criticism; and celebrate the victories along the way.

The Importance of Sharing Your Story

The mind's need to tell the story after a distressing event is like the body's need to spike a fever after an infection. Just as your body seeks to heal and restore itself, so does your mind. You need to tell your story so you can begin integrating your thoughts and emotions.[1] Because you have so many thoughts—some of which are contradictory—and mixed emotions during a time of grief, your mind undertakes a mission to make sense of what's happened to you. Telling your story to others is one way to accomplish that mission.

Telling your story repeatedly to many different people allows you to put all the pieces of your breakup experience together in a coherent whole. Each time you tell your story, new pieces of awareness will come to you as people's questions force you to think of your relational journey and your future in new ways. C. S. Lewis wrote, "You can't see anything properly while your eyes are blurred with tears."[2] Your holy huddle can help you see clearly and get you back on the field so you can go on offense.

Henri Nouwen's qualities of a caring friend also describe characteristics of a holy huddle. A holy huddle is a group of people who, "instead of giving advice, solutions, or cures, have chosen rather to share our pain and touch our wounds with a warm and tender hand . . . can be silent with us in a moment of despair or confusion . . . can stay with us in an hour of grief and bereavement . . . can tolerate not knowing, not curing, not healing and face with us the reality of our powerlessness."[3] Even Jesus had a holy huddle.

Jesus's Holy Huddle

It is commonly known that Jesus had twelve disciples but perhaps not so commonly known that, within the group of twelve, he had an intimate group of three: Peter, James, and John. Jesus was vulnerable with them, inviting them to see him at his best—and at his worst.

He showed his holy huddle his best when he took them up a mountainside and revealed his glory to them. It was as if he were saying to them, "Hey guys, check this out. I want you to be the first to see this." The text says, "His face shone like the sun, and his clothes became as white as the light" (Matt. 17:2). He felt comfortable enough to show them his glory. It takes courage to show people the best side of you without fearing they will judge you or not be willing to enter into your joy.

Jesus also needed his holy huddle when he was at his worst. He took the same three along on his excruciating journey to Gethsemane. *Gethsemane*, ironically, means "olive oil press." Jesus was about to feel the weight and pressure of sorrow in his soul as never before, and he didn't want to be alone. Mark 14:33–34 says, "He took Peter, James and John along with him, and he began to be deeply distressed and troubled. 'My soul is overwhelmed with sorrow to the point of death,' he said to them. 'Stay here and keep watch.'"

Jesus's holy huddle was far from perfect, however. Instead of the disciples standing watch, being alert, and engaging in prayer themselves, when Jesus returned he found them sleeping (Mark 14:37). Nevertheless, Jesus needed his imperfect friends for care, comfort, and support on his epic journey, and so will you.

Practice Your Holy Huddle

For some people, the idea of being vulnerable in a holy huddle conjures up thoughts of throwing an entire package of Sour Patch Kids candy into their mouths. They learned a long time ago that people are sour and hurtful not sweet and safe, and it is better to comfort themselves than risk rejection from others. Brené Brown writes,

> As children we found ways to protect ourselves from vulnerability, from being hurt, diminished, and disappointed. We put on armor; we used our thoughts, emotions, and behaviors as weapons; and we learned how to make ourselves scarce, even to disappear. Now as adults we realize that to live with courage, purpose, and connection—to be the person whom we long to be—we must again be vulnerable. We must take off the armor, put down the weapons, show up, and let ourselves be seen.[4]

Perhaps at one point in your life, armor, walls, and shock absorbers were necessary, but I can promise you they are not going to bring you any lasting comfort or joy. If the thought of reaching out to other people causes you to cringe, I completely understand. Nevertheless, you are meant to be in community. You are biologically wired for intimacy—not meant to live life alone.

It might be time for you to be courageous, take a risk, and commit yourself to practicing being vulnerable with the members of your delicately handpicked holy huddle. Practice reaching out to others, especially if you want to hammer a Do Not Enter sign on the front of your cave and shut yourself inside. Don't travel the road alone. Maybe you think no one will understand you, but it is better to take the risk and find connection and support than to continue alone when Montu takes off at full speed and you get sucked into the vortex of yucky emotions and obsessive negative thoughts.

Make a List

Who feels safe to talk to? Who can you call to say, "Can you come over? I need a hug," or "Hey, I am feeling a little lonely and sad. Can you keep me company on the phone for a little bit?" or "Do you want to hang out and do something fun?" Make a list, and then work it. Find someone who is willing to commit to praying for and checking in on you. Find someone who is not afraid to go scuba diving with you in the deepest, murkiest emotional waters, and someone you can count on to share his or her oxygen if you run out of your own.

If your list turns out to have zero and a half people on it, or if it is difficult for you to take risks and connect with others, then pray that God will bring loving and safe people into your life. God cares for you and your well-being more than you care for yourself. He loves to bring people together to help one another. Psalm 68:6 says, "God sets the lonely in families," and I pray he does that for you.

Expand Your Circle

Maybe you had a big circle of friends and acquaintances before your relationship, but then that circle started shrinking until the only ones left were you and your boyfriend or girlfriend. Maybe love blinded you to the reality of your need for a community or maybe your ex was controlling, jealous, and possessive. Maybe you were just too busy. In any case, now that you have broken up, this is a chance for you to meet new people, join a club, or start your own club.

Jennifer came to see me for therapy. She had definitely been a people person, an extrovert who was comfortable in groups of people. She had loved God and sung on the worship team every other week. Then one day she met Sam.

Sam had come every so often with his friend to check out the hip church with its charismatic pastor and rockin' music. He met Jennifer there and started to come more often. He was definitely interested in her, but she was not as interested in him. He was very persistent and knew all the right words to say. After a while, Jennifer succumbed to his wooing and they started dating.

Jennifer saw some red flags right away. He was a loner and a rebel, and she suspected he might not be as into God as he claimed. Anytime she brought up God, he slyly changed the subject. She had a hunch that maybe Sam was not the best fit for her, but those red flags got lost in the midst of Sam's charm and thoughtfulness. He took her to fancy restaurants in his expensive car and bought her anything she wanted.

With time, Sam told Jennifer he didn't like some of her friends and asked her not to hang out with them. Apparently, he thought some of the guys liked her. Jennifer agreed not to hang out with that group of people because she loved Sam. Her church attendance began to decrease as well, because Sam liked to take her out on the weekends. Missing church and her community became a habit.

When Sam finally broke Jennifer's heart and left her for someone else, she no longer had her support system and was left to carry her broken heart all by herself. As her therapist, I helped her grieve the loss of her relationship and encouraged her to reach out to loved ones. When the blur of her past year and a half with Sam cleared, she once again realized how important friends and family were. She said to me, "I can't believe that was me, isolating myself, living only for Sam, and doing what he wanted. I lost myself. But now God has been so gracious to me, and I could never have made it without reaching out to my friends and family for support. They took me back with open arms and open hearts and have become a life jacket in this torturous storm of grief."

Maybe you had a large circle of friends but walked away from it. Or maybe you still have a circle of friends, but could use a couple more people in it. Practice openness, vulnerability, and honesty with a few people you trust. God never meant for any of us to do life alone. Find your holy huddle and enjoy it for a lifetime.

CHAPTER 11

Heal: Deal, Feel, Reveal, Seal
(DFRS)

*In confession the light of the Gospel breaks
into the darkness and seclusion of the heart.*
—Dietrich Bonhoeffer, *Life Together*

Mitch was devastated after losing his girlfriend. But he didn't want to appear weak around his other friends, so he tried brushing off his pain. Anytime his girlfriend's name came up in conversations, he laughed it off. "Yeah, well, it is her loss. She is the one missing out," he said, using the shock absorbers of denial and intellectualization (using reasoning to avoid difficult emotions). All the while, he deeply grieved his loss.

He didn't want to experience what he knew deep inside about his loss. So he worked longer hours and drank at bars more often, trying to cover up the pain. Over many months, he started getting really bad headaches and didn't hang out as much with his friends. He would come home from work, eat a little something, and go to bed. Some days he felt so heavy that he started calling in sick at work. He didn't know exactly what was wrong, but he knew he needed help, so he reached out to me for counseling.

Mitch could deny and suppress his emotions for only so long. With time, the weight of his swirling emotions took its toll on his soul. I helped him grieve well by walking him through a four-step process I developed to help people heal emotionally. We'll get to the rest of his story later in the chapter. For now, I want to walk you through the same process I took Mitch through. For you to heal from an overwhelming, negative, and constricting emotional state, you have to deal, feel, reveal, and seal (DFRS).

Deal

The first step in the process is to make the choice to deal with your aching heart. In John 5, Jesus was in Jerusalem at the pool of Bethesda, or pool of *mercy* as it is translated, where there were people with all kinds of ailments. As Jesus walked around, he encountered a man who had been ill for thirty-eight years. The first question Jesus asked him was, "Do you want to get well?" I believe Jesus asks all of us this question when we suffer emotionally.

Whether we want to get well may not always be an easy question to answer. Dealing can be costly. Healing is much better than remaining in emotional turmoil, but there is always a cost to the ego—that part of us that likes to protect and hold on to the status quo for fear of losing our identity. Dealing causes us to feel things we don't want to feel, think about things we would much rather forget, or change behaviors we don't want to change.

The man's ego could have prompted him to say to Jesus, "Um, I have been sick for a long time; it is now my identity. If I give it up, I will somehow lose who I am as a sick person and all the attention as well. Thanks but no thanks." Choosing to deal with your aching heart and declaring you want to get well is the first step to jettisoning your emotional baggage.

Feel

The second step is to allow yourself to feel. This step calls you to be present with your anger, sadness, fear, anxiety, and any other overwhelming emotions you might experience, instead of using shock absorbers to avoid them.

The major task of this step is to set aside time to face your feelings before God, the ultimate revealer of truth, which will bring clarity to your experience. Don't be afraid. God loves it when we are truthful, no matter how ugly we think our experiences may be. And he much prefers that to seeing us wearing a mask—pretending and bearing false witness. God can't heal our masks because they are inanimate objects, but God can heal an authentic hurting soul that is laid bare before him.

The authors of *How to Survive the Loss of a Love* encourage those in pain from a traumatic breakup to feel deeply and fully embrace their inner experiences. They write: "Don't postpone, deny, cover, or run from your pain. Be with it now. Everything else can wait. An emotional wound requires the same priority treatment as a physical wound. Set aside time to mourn. The sooner you allow yourself to be with your pain, the sooner it will pass; the only way out is through. Feel the fear, pain, desolation, and anger. It's essential to the healing process. You are alive. You will survive."[1]

Although the use of shock absorbers may seem helpful at first, the ongoing practice guarantees that you will have unwelcome side effects, and you will, eventually, still have to come to terms with your emotional pain. Lysa Terkeurst, the author of *Unglued: Making Wise Choices in the Midst of Raw Emotions*, writes, "Stuffing means pushing emotions inward. We swallow hard and lock our hurt feelings inside, not in an effort to process and release them, but to wallow in the hurt. Much like an oyster deals with the irritation of a grain of sand, we coat the issue with more and more layers of hurt until it forms a hard rock of sorts." She continues, "But this rock is no pearl. It's a rock that we'll eventually use either to build a barrier or to hurl at someone else in retaliation."[2]

Suppressing your feelings is like pushing an inflated beach ball underwater. Eventually it will burst back up with greater force than it took to push it down. If you're not careful, the ball will hit you or others in the face. Deal with your emotions now so they won't forcefully pop up, like the beach ball, somewhere else in your life.

What emotional pain you resist will persist and over time can become an unwelcome hindrance to experiencing life to the fullest. Allowing yourself to feel will be instrumental in grieving well and will be an invaluable skill that will benefit you for a lifetime.

Throughout the ages, saints of old have laid bare their emotional landscapes before the Lord. In Psalm 31:9, the psalmist says, "Be merciful to me, LORD, for I am in *distress*; my eyes grow weak with *sorrow*, my soul and body with *grief*" (emphasis mine). It was said of Hannah, "In her deep anguish Hannah prayed to the LORD, weeping bitterly" (1 Sam. 1:10). In Romans 9:2, the apostle Paul says, "I have great *sorrow* and unceasing *anguish* in my heart" (emphasis mine). Even Jesus was not afraid to be vulnerable. How can we forget his excruciating cry, "My God, my God, why have you forsaken me?" (Matt. 27:46). *At some point*, we will all feel pain, suffering, sorrow, anger, and grief. So give yourself permission to feel deeply. As the old adage says, "Keep it real."

Reveal

In order to heal, the most powerful, yet admittedly the scariest, thing to do is to reveal your emotional experience to a compassionate, empathic other—the third step. Although it takes risk and courage to be vulnerable and allow others into the inner sanctum of your heart, the rewards completely outweigh the risks. It is healthier to reveal your emotions when you share with the right person than to perpetually conceal them.

Who can you choose to safely reveal your experience to? God, a friend, a pastor, a therapist, or someone else you trust to have an empathetic listening ear and a wise and nonjudgmental heart would all be good choices.

Seal

The last step is to *seal*. To complete the practice of healing from overwhelming and painful emotions and rabble-rousing thoughts, give yourself over to the seal of the compassionate, empathic response of your confidant.

Have you ever heard of a product called WoundSeal? Let's say someone accidentally cuts his hand preparing the fishing line on a boating trip, and he begins to bleed profusely. He desperately needs stitches, but the hospital is many miles away. WoundSeal to the rescue! WoundSeal is a special powder clinically proven to seal wounds and stop bleeding instantly. It has been a lifesaver for many. The compassionate and loving responses of others are similar to WoundSeal in that they cover emotional wounds and hurting people heal faster.

Seal—the last step of the DFRS process, occurs when you surrender to the loving response of another person. Whether they give you a touch, a hug, a word of encouragement, or a loving challenge, those to whom you reveal your pain can close the gaping wound, allowing greater levels of healing to occur. Many times, the best seal someone can give is an offering of presence, where words fall away and compassion is still deeply felt.

Give yourself the gift of the compassionate, loving presence of another as many times as your wound opens up and oozes pain and discomfort. Rarely is there a single-shot treatment for sorrow. Healing is more of a process and journey than a one-stop shop.

Take a Break

Before we continue with Mitch's story, I want you to know that there may be times when instead of going inward, you may need to go outward. I spend a lot of time throughout this book asking you to go inward because there is so much gold to mine there, and such mining can lead to nuggets of healing and transformation. But sometimes too much analysis can cause paralysis. If you start to engage in DFRS, or other intense practices, and it feels too overwhelming, then take your mind off yourself and your situation for a while. Go out and have some fun. Watch a movie. Go surfing. Worship God. Or go to the mountains and wonder over God's creation.

Mitch's Story

When Mitch had finally had enough, he chose to deal with his emotions by coming to see me. It took a while for him to start talking about his emotions, but he made the choice to feel them and started sharing and revealing the full impact of his loss—his anger, sadness, doubt, and grief. I was profoundly touched by his openness and honesty. I provided a seal for Mitch's wound by creating a safe, accepting atmosphere, fulfilling Paul's call in Galatians 6:2 to "carry each other's burdens, and in this way you will fulfill the law of Christ." Mitch found this four-step process to be transformative, not only in the counseling room but also outside with people he trusted.

Allowing the deal, feel, reveal, and seal (DFRS) process to

bring healing from your traumatic emotional experiences can help you not only to recover from heartbreak but also to traverse the rest of the valleys you will inevitably experience in life. May it be one practice that you can use for your emotional and spiritual health among many in your arsenal.

CHAPTER 12

Journaling

Journal writing is a voyage to the interior.
—CHRISTINA BALDWIN, *One to One*

W here I come from, we need to be wary of stagnant pools of water. Over time, because of the location and high humidity, they become discolored and smelly. They also become a breeding ground for weird and unsightly insects—including nasty, blood-sucking mosquitoes that especially enjoy snacking on people.

The same thing happens when all your anger, sadness, shame, and pain remain stagnant and unprocessed. If those emotions sit in your soul and are not processed, your soul can become a breeding ground for nasty critters like self-doubt, bitterness, unforgiveness, and hate, and eventually become a pond of depression. This is why journaling is essential. Journaling is a practice that helps you take what is on the inside and bring it into the light on the outside. It keeps your inner world moving, flowing like a vibrant and lively river, rather than an icky and murky pond.

Journaling is a powerful practice you can use to help you grieve well, heal your delicate heart, and gain transformative insights into your past, present, and future. Studies have shown that expressing yourself through writing can reduce the symptoms of depression and anxiety, improve your mood, and increase your immune system and overall physical health.[1] One study in particular, which looked at the effects of journaling after a romantic breakup, concluded, "In the aftermath of a failed relationship, expressive writing reduced individuals' risk for developing symptoms of upper respiratory illness, tension and fatigue."[2]

Late at night when everyone is sleeping, except you because you're struggling with insomnia, or at times when you still feel like you cannot confide in someone else, even in the daytime when everyone's awake, your journal can become a sounding board and a powerful instrument for healing.

Your Emotional Suitcase

Imagine a movie scene where a character is packing for a trip. In a rush to leave, he throws everything into his suitcase, wrestles it closed, and runs toward the door. But the bulging suitcase hits the door frame on the way out and busts open, sending its contents flying out. The same thing can happen with our emotional suitcases.

When you first experience a breakup, you are devastated. You feel as if your whole world has exploded and lies in pieces on the dirty floor. So you try to cope by shoving many of your thoughts and emotions down into your overflowing suitcase (the unconscious) to deal with later. Unfortunately, since it is over-packed with stuff (negative thoughts and emotions), your emotional suitcase will fly open if you bump it against something (triggers—such as hearing about your ex being with someone else), and your stuff will fly out (impatience toward others, angry outbursts, etc.). Many people quickly pick up their T-shirts (negative thoughts), jeans (anger), and underwear (grief) and try to cram them back inside the suitcase, but this process can occur over and over until you either get rid of some items or pack them in a different way.

Journaling enables you to unpack your emotional luggage.[3] It can help you pay attention to what is going on in your innermost being and help you separate and label feelings of guilt, loss, anger, and sadness. Once you label your emotions, your nervous system gradually calms down and you start to feel a little more sane and relaxed. That is just how we are wired. We like to make sense of things. We like things in order and in neat little packages. It makes us feel safer and more secure.

After a period of prayerfully packing, unpacking, and repacking through journaling, you will find you no longer need those holey jeans and stained T-shirts, so you can donate them to the red cross. I am not referring to the humanitarian organization, but Jesus's blood-stained cross from two thousand years ago. Jesus's act of love on that red cross forever opened the way for us to "approach God's throne of grace with confidence, so that we may receive mercy and find grace to help us in our time of need" (Heb. 4:16). Journaling can become a prayerful practice through which you can cast "all your cares [all your anxieties, all your worries, and all your concerns, once and for all] on Him, for He cares about you [with deepest affection, and watches over you very carefully]" (1 Peter 5:7 AMP).

How to Keep a Journal

Long before there was scientific research, there were countless people, from every tribe and tongue, keeping journals as a spiritual and emotional healing practice. King David was one of them. The lovesick psalmist was a master at grieving well, partly because, as a trauma survivor, he kept a journal to share his heart, to grieve, and to think about things he understood only when he wrote them down. As a form of prayer, journaling became a way for him to approach God's throne of grace and communicate deeply with him. Let's look at one of David's psalms to get some ideas for what you can write about in your journal.

How long, LORD? Will you forget me forever?
　　How long will you hide your face from me?
How long must I wrestle with my thoughts
　　and day after day have sorrow in my heart?
　　How long will my enemy triumph over me?

Look on me and answer, LORD my God.
　　Give light to my eyes, or I will sleep in death,
and my enemy will say, "I have overcome him,"
　　and my foes will rejoice when I fall.

But I trust in your unfailing love;
　　my heart rejoices in your salvation.
I will sing the LORD's praise,
　　for he has been good to me.

(Ps. 13)

Questions Are Encouraged

You can include questions while you journal. It can be difficult and scary for us to admit that we don't have all the answers, but having questions presupposes that we don't have answers. People are prone to stick with the answers they have because of the comfort and security answers bring, even if they don't believe those answers. The key to journaling, however, is honesty, knowing that God loves truth and knows that the truth—in all its forms—will set us free.

When David asked questions—"Will you forget me?" and "How long [a phrase he says four times] will you hide your face from me?"—it was an acknowledgment that at least a part of him was afraid that God had forgotten him or was somehow hiding.

That could be scary to admit for someone like David who loved God and praised him that his presence is everywhere (Ps. 139:8).

Like David, allow questions to be part of your writing practice. Questions such as "Where are you, God?" "How long do I have to suffer?" "Why did the breakup have to happen?" and "Why did you allow me to have the relationship in the first place?" are all fair game. Include whatever questions come to mind in the moment. And you never know, you could look back at the journal in a few months and be amazed at how God answered some of them.

Include Emotions

Include emotions in your journal. David's distress was obvious in Psalm 13; his emotions were oozing out everywhere. In fact, he specifically named "sorrow" as one of his painful emotions in verse 2. The Hebrew word for *sorrow* signifies a deep grief and inner torment. According to verse 3, David felt as if he was going to die: "Give light to my eyes, or I will sleep in death."

I don't think he was really going to die, but that was how he felt. By the way, David uses words like this quite often in his psalms (Pss.18; 22; 23; 94; and 116). You might also feel that way sometimes. When you are experiencing extreme emotions that don't make sense, write about them. Your journal is a place for you to write out and name your emotions.

What if you sit down to write in your journal, and you can't discern your emotions? I needed help discerning mine in the beginning. Emotion charts, which are pictures of different emotional facial expressions, are really helpful for those who don't know what they feel. Free charts can be found online and printed out. Many of my clients have used them and tell me they have helped.

When you don't know what is going on inside, go to the One who does. John 16:13 says, "But when he, the Spirit of truth, comes, he will guide you into all the truth." Ask God to shine his flashlight into your heart so you can clearly identify what you're thinking and feeling. Ask God to reveal those areas of pain in your heart that are affecting you so deeply. Pray, "Holy Spirit, I don't understand what is going on with me. In your gentle and loving way, will you help me figure it out?" The Holy Spirit loves to unveil and reveal truth so you can walk in the way everlasting.

Share Requests

When you journal, include requests. In Psalm 13:3–4, David writes, "Look on me and answer, LORD my God. Give light to my eyes, or I will sleep in death, and my enemy will say, 'I have overcome him,' and my foes will rejoice when I fall." I love the drama of it all. David is basically praying, "Lord, you better show up and answer me, or I am going to die. And if you don't show up, the people I hate the most will make fun of me."

Write in your journal and ask God for whatever you need. One heartbroken friend of mine shared how she didn't hold anything back while journaling. She wrote things like, "God, please smite that son of a [not a nice word]," and "God, please send me someone like Brad Pitt for my next boyfriend." Asking doesn't mean God is going to hunt down and smite your ex or give you a Brad Pitt or a Jennifer Lawrence for your next partner. The point here is to be honest with God, even if what you tell him sounds a little far-out.

Self-Compassion Journaling

Self-compassion journaling has helped many people get through difficult times. This journaling exercise uses the components of self-compassion—mindfulness, common humanity, and kindness—to process everyday events in a compassionate and loving way. This type of writing, when bathed in prayer, can be an incredible practice to use throughout the rest of your life to work through troublesome everyday events.

Mindfulness

At the end of a long day, in the quiet of the night when the technology is turned off, review your day's journey. Journal any difficult or painful experiences you had to deal with during the day. Pay especially close attention to those events that are weighing heavily on your conscience, those incidents that cause you to feel bad about yourself or that you've judged yourself for. As you reflect on those experiences, write how you feel about them. Take notice of how your physiology is affected as you're processing each event. For example, notice where you feel tension in your body or whether your breathing is deep or shallow. Where the Spirit of the Lord is, there is freedom, so engage in this exercise without being harsh with yourself.

At some point during the day, you might have begged and pleaded with your ex to come back when you knew you shouldn't have. After processing the event, you notice you're angry with yourself—you feel some energy in your stomach, and your jaw has tightened a bit. Write about all of that.

Or perhaps you didn't accomplish anything all day, and now you're feeling tired and depressed. As you are mindful about the day, you notice you feel shame. As you're writing about this experience, you notice you have less energy and your posture is slightly slumped. This is how you process, notice, and journal the experience.

Common Humanity

The next step would be to write about how your experiences are common to other people's experiences, thinking especially about heartbroken people whose relationships have ended. This step connects you with the rest of humanity and is an acknowledgment that "there is nothing new under the sun" (Eccl. 1:9). This type of journaling can revolve around the common experience of loss, sadness, or grief. You might journal about unwise decisions that you and countless others have made in similar circumstances.

Self-Kindness or Self-Compassion

In this step, you can either write down compassionate words found in the Bible, as if they were written to you (they were), or write down kind and encouraging words from your compassionate self. Proverbs 18:21 says, "The tongue has the power of life and death." Words have tremendous power. Coming from God, others, or yourself, words can either gently lift you out of a dark pit or violently throw you into one. They can bring life or death.

Perhaps you felt death from the words of someone you loved who said, "I am sorry; it is over between us," or experienced that feeling when a parent said you were no good or that you will never amount to anything. On the other hand, maybe you've experienced life from loving words of encouragement, such as, "You are the best thing that ever happened to me," or "I am proud of you." Proverbs 16:24 says, "Gracious words are a honeycomb, sweet to the soul and healing to the bones." The power of words is amazing!

Putting the Self-Compassion Pieces Together

Let's apply this section using the hypothetical event in which you begged your ex to come back. You noticed that you were angry with yourself because you allowed yourself to be weak and vulnerable and you went against your desire to never contact your ex again. You connected your experience with similar experiences from others. And now you're ready to write yourself a word of kindness and compassion from the Scriptures.

You might personalize Jeremiah 29:11. Even though the context is very different from yours, the message remains the same. You could journal something like this: "God loves me and knows the plans he has for me. God will prosper me and not harm me and will give me hope and a future." Or you can combine and personalize verses like Ephesians 1:4 and Colossians 3:12 like this: "God, I am yours. You chose me before the creation of the world. I am holy and dearly loved. Even though I get angry with myself, help me to clothe myself with compassion, kindness, humility, gentleness, and patience. Help me to be patient with myself as I go through these dark and uncharted grieving territories. Help me forgive myself as you have already forgiven me."

Ending your journal entry with self-compassion and kindness toward yourself is a powerful practice. You are declaring the loving truth of God over your life. Doing so over time will strengthen your spirit and definitely help you grieve well.

Just Write Anything

Finally, it's important to remember that as you begin your journaling journey, you might fumble and stumble for words. Susan Duke, author of *Grieving Forward*, writes, "At times, my journal provided the only place I could tell all and spill my tears recklessly. The first journal is filled with ink-smeared pages from the torrent of tears that fell as I wrote the only truths I knew at that moment. A poorly scrawled question, an obvious objection, or one Scripture—accompanied at times by a question mark—often took up one whole page. But those scribblings reflected the cries of my heart."[4]

You may first sit staring at a blank page for half an hour not knowing what to write. But even if it is one word, one scribble, or one small sentiment, begin to write, and experience the many benefits of the practice of journaling.

CHAPTER 13

Shut the Front Door

*Close some doors today. Not because of
pride, incapacity or arrogance, but simply
because they no longer lead somewhere.*
—Paulo Coelho

Throughout history, a door has been used in metaphors to signify various things: pathways into transformative religious knowledge ("Seek and you will find; knock and the door will be opened to you"—Matt. 7:7), the opening up of new opportunities (The door opened for me to get that job!), the end of one's options (The door of opportunity closed on that new deal), passageways into fairy-tale lands (C. S. Lewis's *The Lion, the Witch and the Wardrobe*), and portals into parallel universes (*Monsters, Inc.*). Did you know that you have a front door to your heart?

Jesus says, "Here I am! I stand at the door and knock. If anyone hears my voice and opens the door, I will come in and eat with that person, and they with me" (Rev. 3:20). Jesus is referring to a symbolic door to our hearts. The "door" is the pathway to the innermost part of who we are, the inner sanctum where our mind, will, and emotions reside.

We already talked about vertical pathway practices, such as prayer, that encourage you to *open* the front door of your heart.

Now we will discuss two practices that will encourage you to *close* the front door of your heart for the sake of healing. The first practice is shutting the door to your ex, and the second practice is shutting the door to that which tries to sabotage God's healing in your life—sin.

Shut the Front Door to Your Ex

I imagine Jesus's knocks sound like gentle whispers, like this: "I love you. I long to be present with you. Will you let me in?" It is always a good idea to let Jesus in. Unfortunately, Jesus is not the only one knocking and desiring to come into your precious home. Even after the breakup, it is common for the ex to slyly try to get back together or for the griever to pretend to shut the door but leave it open, unconsciously hoping for an ex-lover's return.

The imperfect, but very wise man Solomon has some good advice for those who intend to leave the door open to their ex, even if it is only a crack. He writes, "Above all else, guard your heart, for everything you do flows from it" (Prov. 4:23).

Maybe you are a hopeless romantic and want to maintain a glimmer of hope for getting back with your ex. For the sake of your healing process, here is my advice: Guard your heart. Shut the front door. It is over. Even if your ex told you that he or she needed to break up with you just long enough to gain some time or space, close the door. It is better to surrender to the reality before you than to perpetuate the fantasy. If, for whatever reason, you and your ex decide it feels right to be together down the road, you can deal with that situation if and when it arises. But for now, shut the door.

Closing the door to your ex could also be the best thing for your future partner. Assuming God has not called you to celibacy for the rest of your life, you might want to allow what is left of your tender heart to heal so you have more to give in your next romantic relationship. Do not let your ex, most likely the person who has chosen not to be with you, take from your heart and your future partner any more than he or she already has. For the sake of your heart and your grieving process, let your ex go.

What Leaving the Door Open Looks Like

In order to confirm that you have closed the door to your heart, let's look at what leaving it open looks like. Looking at old photographs when the two of you were lovey-dovey is a sure sign that you're keeping the door open. Staying connected on Facebook and browsing your ex's wall to see what he or she is up to and who he or she is hanging out with is another clear sign that you're keeping the door open. So is engaging in emotional drunk texting (EDT). EDT doesn't necessarily have anything to do with alcohol. It just refers to a loss of control over rational faculties (prefrontal cortex) because of the intoxicating influences of anxiety, loneliness, and sadness (activated amygdala). Because the emotions are so overwhelming, the person desperately throws rationality out the window and texts his or her ex for comfort or acknowledgment.

Leaving the Door Open Prolongs Your Grief

The more you open the door and invite your ex back in, the longer it will take you to grieve, heal, and move on. In a recent study, for example, researchers wanted to find out if continuing to look at an ex's Facebook page actually kept heartbroken people from recovering and moving on.[1] After examining data from 464 participants, they found "exposure to an ex-partner through Facebook may obstruct the process of healing and moving on from a past relationship."[2]

Constantly looking at pictures and Facebook, sending texts, reminiscing, and ruminating about your ex will trigger emotional memories of the two of you as a couple and ultimately keep the romantic emotional fires burning longer than necessary. Not only could the above prolong your grief process, but you could be so busy thinking about your ex that you could miss out on other opportunities. Helen Keller wrote, "When one door of happiness closes, another opens; but often we look so long at the closed door that we do not see the one which has been opened for us." When you keep the door open to your ex, it is hard to see what new doors God is opening all around you.

Letting Go Is Hard

Letting go and shutting the front door to your heart is easier said than done. As I reflect on my breakup from years ago, I am reminded of how hard it was. I remember trying to fight for my ex for a few months. Honestly, I think it was more like harassing or begging her. I refused to let go. I thought that if I did not give up but fought valiantly for her, she would magically come back because of my persistence. The reality was, the longer I chained myself to the past, the longer I stunted my grieving process and kept God's best for me from arriving.

It took me a while, but I began to practice shutting the front door. I got rid of the pictures. I just couldn't believe that my future partner would appreciate looking at them, and it would be too easy to pick them up and start reminiscing again when I felt lonely. Every time I felt the urge to look at our mutual friends' Facebook pages to see if she wrote something about me, I remembered the practice of shutting the front door. No more texting my ex, begging God to bring her back, or asking friends if she was seeing someone. I decided to guard my heart, let go, and do a trust fall into the gentle but strong arms of an amazing

God. My prayer, admittedly reluctant at times, was, "Fine, God. You win. Not my will but your will be done."

After I accepted the finality of the breakup, my healing process skyrocketed. I allowed God full access to do what he wanted to do in my heart, and I submitted to his will and the will of my ex-girlfriend. I didn't fight reality anymore and live in the fantasy of what could be. I closed the door completely.

Over time I started to see new doors open all around me. They were doors of new adventures, new friends, and new opportunities for growth. And eventually, many years later after dozens of invaluable lessons had been learned, I found a new romantic partner, who eventually became my wife.

Although I don't remember where I heard this saying, it spoke powerfully to me at the time of my breakup: "It is hard to let go of the good that you know, to receive God's greater good that you don't know." It is so true. Letting go of the affectionate touches, warm hugs, and passionate words that you and your ex spoke to one another is hard. But if you are going to receive God's greater good for your life, you must surrender, let go, and shut the front door.

Shut the Front Door to Sin

It started off as an average morning for a loving family in Pennsylvania. The husband was getting ready for work while his wife was upstairs taking care of the household, and their delightful son was sleeping. He decided to let their lively dog outside. He left the door open knowing the dog would finish his morning frolicking and come back in when he was done. A few minutes later, the dog did come back inside, but unfortunately, a black bear followed him.

The ferocious bear started to maul the man. When his wife came downstairs to investigate the commotion, the bear attacked her too. The man, through sheer will, got the beast off his wife and watched it flee back into the woods. Afterward, the couple was in desperate need of medical attention and their house was a bloody mess. They learned many lessons that day; one of them was to be cautious about leaving the door open because you never know what danger might come inside and wreak havoc.

You can be in such a vulnerable place after your breakup. Your self-esteem has taken a nasty blow, and you may feel that you are not worthy of anyone's love. Depression, hopelessness, and a mountain of negative emotions can feel like an avalanche waiting to crush you. Because of your feelings, you might be tempted to leave the door of your heart open, and, knowingly or unknowingly, invite dangerous predators inside.

Genesis 4:7 says, "If you do what is right, will you not be accepted? But if you do not do what is right, sin is crouching at your door; it desires to have you, but you must rule over it." Sin and false lovers look to see if your door is open ever so slightly. When it is, they come knocking and whispering sweet nothings in your ear, hoping you will let them in. They say,

"Hey, you want a quick fix?"

"I can distract you and make you feel good. You don't have to tell anybody."

"You have been feeling like garbage for a while now. This is your time to let loose and be free."

"Has God really said that this is bad for you? I don't think that is the case. You're in pain. Take my hand and let's go."

Sin is anything that ruptures, fractures, wounds, distorts, and numbs your relationship with God, self, and others. Sexy sin wants you to come out and play, promising to help you forget about the pain. Sin disguised as religion, for example, knocks at the door and says, "If you give me all your time and energy, and if you work really hard, you will be loved more and God will certainly give you a sense of his presence." Pornography comes around the corner and says, "Hey, lonesome, I will show you a good time and fill your emptiness." And when your loneliness becomes unbearable, persuasive people suddenly pop up out of nowhere, wanting to comfort you in the wrong kinds of ways. (As an aside, be careful—rebound relationships rarely work out.) The longer we allow sin to creep into our hearts and take up residence, the more it can lead to patterns of idolatry.

First John 5:21 says, "Dear children, keep yourselves from idols." Idols are glorified baby bottles. Idolatry can be a pattern of looking for comfort and security in things, people, and places that are outside of God's design for your life. Continually seeking comfort from friends and family when you are down in the dumps is not idolatrous because it is God's design and purpose for us to love and be loved by one another. Engaging in a pattern of getting blitzed with a bottle of vodka three days a week is opening the door to a ferocious bear waiting to ravage you. Getting drunk is not in God's original design or purpose for your life when you need comforting; therefore, it is an idol.

Sin and idolatrous behavior will maul and kill you, but unlike the bear in the story above, they can only come in when invited. When you hear them creeping around, guard your heart, cling to Christ, and shut the front door.

The Guard, Par Excellence

If I were a wealthy man and had something precious to protect, like a $54 million gem, and was fearful someone might come and steal it, I would hide it behind a huge steel door and hire a guard to protect it 24-7. I would make sure the guard was built like the actor Dwayne "The Rock" Johnson and had the fighting skills of mixed martial artist "Rowdy" Ronda Rousey. Believe it or not, you have something more expensive and precious than a glittering gem—your heart. Although you probably could not afford Johnson or Rousey to protect you 24-7, I know of someone who could take them on with one hand tied behind his back and who would be willing to stand guard at no cost to you. His name is Jesus.

In Philippians 4:6–7, Paul says, "Do not be anxious about anything, but in every situation, by prayer and petition, with thanksgiving, present your requests to God. And the peace of God, which transcends all understanding, will guard your hearts and your minds in Christ Jesus." These verses teach us who the best person to guard our hearts is—Jesus. We know from the Scriptures that Jesus is the "Prince of Peace" (Isa. 9:6). It is a simple task to get him to stand guard. Set a time to talk to God (prayer), ask him for what you need (petition), and marinate your time with an attitude of gratitude (thanksgiving). When the beauty of Christ is standing guard at the door of your fragile heart, you become less vulnerable to unhealthy, or flat-out destructive, forces in your life.

Learning to shut the front door of your heart when you are tempted to reach out to your ex or to sin will take practice. Sometimes you will succeed and other times you will not. Know that you don't have to do it alone. Jesus will not only help you guard your heart but also give you the grace and power you need to say no to temptation in its various forms.

CHAPTER 14

Forgive to Live

*As I walked out the door toward the gate that would
lead to my freedom, I knew if I didn't leave my bitterness
and hatred behind, I'd still be in prison.*
—NELSON MANDELA

Laura was deeply angry at her ex-boyfriend Joshua for using her for her money and her body and then eventually dumping her. She said she had given to him, even at times when she didn't want to, because she loved him and believed he loved her. She held on to unforgiveness for quite a while. Every time she heard his name, she seethed with anger. One day, I brought up forgiveness and she became furious with me for even mentioning it.

"I am not letting him off the hook!" she said. "Don't bring that word up right now!"

I didn't blame her. Joshua had done some pretty nasty things to her. But eventually, she would have to choose either to stay bitter or to get better. If she didn't choose to get better and allow the poison to get out of her system, she and those she spent time with would reap some consequences. Unfortunately, for a while, she chose to stay bitter.

Eventually Laura started dating again, and the effects of her unwillingness to forgive spilled into her new relationship. When her new boyfriend was late, she became distrustful and berated him. If, occasionally, he asked for a favor, she quickly accused him of trying to use her. These incidents left him bewildered, and he got defensive and upset, which, to Laura, confirmed that her new boyfriend was a jerk. She lashed out at him, he lashed back, and round and round they went.

The new boyfriend certainly had some issues and contributed to their pattern of disconnection, but because Laura had never dealt with the injury Joshua had inflicted on her, she harbored unforgiveness. This unforgiveness became a wound that adversely affected her new relationship. If we don't deal with our unresolved emotional issues, someone else will inevitably pay the price.

What Forgiveness Is and Is Not

Forgiveness is *not* forgetting, pretending, or a fancy word for psychological suppression. It is not becoming a doormat for verbal or physical abusers. Forgiveness is certainly not keying your ex's car and leaving a black rose on the windshield. Forgiving your ex does not mean you will never feel the sting of the rejection again or any residue of anger. And forgiveness is not the green light that invites your ex to come hold your hand and work his or her way back into your heart, although God could certainly call you to reconciliation.

Forgiveness *is* a prayerful process of surrendering to God's will and making a choice to release the debt we feel the injurer owes us because of how deeply he or she hurt us. True forgiveness does not deny but accepts the full impact of the injuring partner's choices and makes a decision to let go and let God perform his transformational work in our lives. Forgiveness is also a powerful gift from God that releases us from the poison of the bitterness of unforgiveness.

God did not command us to forgive to make life hard but to emancipate us from a hard life and propel us toward a future where love is easily expressed and felt. The apostle Paul lovingly encourages us to "make every effort to live in peace with everyone" (Heb. 12:14) and cautions us "that no bitter root grows up to cause trouble and defile many" (v. 15). If we choose to harbor the bitter root and negative energy of unforgiveness, then we are wasting additional energy to keep those destructive elements at bay so they don't spill out and harm ourselves and other people. But what if you forgave, released yourself from the negative energy, and instead used the freed-up emotional energy in positive ways? That energy could be used to love yourself, God, and others with much greater capacity. There is no greater joy than to love and be loved freely!

Process of Forgiveness

Everett Worthington, Christian psychologist and counselor, dedicated his life to studying forgiveness after someone raped and murdered his mother. He developed a five-step model of forgiveness, which beautifully portrays what forgiveness looks like.[1] The following is his acrostic **REACH:**

1. **R**ecall the hurt
2. **E**mpathize with the one who hurt you
3. **A**ltruistic gift of forgiveness, offer
4. **C**ommitment to forgive, make
5. **H**old on to the forgiveness

These steps are not meant to be a cookie-cutter approach to forgiveness, but rather a helpful guide for practicing and increasing our ability to forgive.

The first step is to *recall* the hurt and injury. In other words, fully enter into the details of the event, including the hurt, pain, and sadness. Think about what your ex said, did, or didn't say or do, that caused you pain. You could also try writing the story out, starting when you met, moving on to how the breakup occurred, and ending with how you presently feel toward the injurer.

Second, *empathize* and meditate upon what the other person might have been going through that would move him or her to hurt you. What do you think was going on in your ex's life, heart, and mind at the time? What dynamics in his or her childhood would cause him or her to act in certain ways in the present? Think about times when you might have hurt someone in a similar way. As hard as it might be, try to place yourself in the other person's shoes and understand what his or her life was like before the hurtful event (or events) happened.

Third, extend the *altruistic* gift of forgiveness to the other person (and yourself). Let go of the debt you believe your ex owes you. This usually takes time, and it can be one of the hardest steps to do. It could be an exercise of your will at first, but at some point your emotions will follow.

If you need help accomplishing this step, start by remembering a time when you hurt someone else and how it felt when that person forgave you. If you continue to struggle, start praying for your ex. With time and the grace of God, you will eventually be able to let go of your resentment and forgive.

The fourth step is to make a *commitment* to the forgiveness you've extended to your ex and make that decision known to others, whether it is by sharing it with your holy huddle or with your ex. If seeing the person is too risky, write a letter to him or her or write a letter to yourself in your journal. Symbolize your decision to forgive in some tangible way; plant a tree, find a special rock and make it a memorial stone, or make a certificate. Use your imagination.

Lastly, *hold* on to the forgiveness you purposed in your heart, especially when old memories and painful feelings rise to the surface. One day you can go through the steps, find tremendous peace, and believe you have forgiven your ex. Then, only days later, you may be angered by a memory and believe that your original forgiveness didn't work or was not real. Max Lucado writes, "Forgiveness vacillates like this. It has fits and starts, good days and bad. Anger intermingled with love. Irregular mercy. We make progress only to make a wrong turn. Step forward and fall back. But this is okay. When it comes to forgiveness, all of us are beginners."[2] When you are struggling to forgive, that is a time to hold on to the forgiveness you have initially committed to, trusting God to help you complete the process in due time.

Just so you know, there are really good reasons for why it seems you have forgiven your ex one day only to have feelings of anger and revenge well up three days later. Neuroscientists differentiate between the higher region of the brain (neocortex) and the lower regions (reptilian and limbic systems). Your feelings resurface not because you haven't forgiven your partner but because painful memories deeply encoded within your nervous system and lower regions of the brain have not yet caught up to your will, which is in the higher region. In other words, it takes time for your heart (the seat of your emotions) to catch up with your mind (the logic and rational faculties).

Prayerfully go through the REACH steps again if you need to, as well as the DFRS process, while engaging in self-compassion, knowing that most people struggle with forgiveness.

Research on Forgiveness and Unforgiveness

In a recent research study on forgiveness, participants were randomly assigned one of two conditions: either forgiveness or unforgiveness.[3] Those assigned to forgiveness were asked to write about a time when they were seriously offended by someone and chose to forgive them. Those who were assigned the unforgiveness condition wrote about a time when they were seriously offended but chose not to forgive.

Both sets of participants then engaged in two experiments. In the first experiment the participants examined a hill for steepness and gauged the difficulty in climbing it. The researchers observed the difference, if any, in the groups' visual perceptions of the hill's geographical slant. In the second experiment participants jumped five times without bending their knees, and the researchers measured the difference between the heights the groups achieved.

In the first experiment, those participants who had forgiven viewed the hill as less steep than did those who had not forgiven. In the second activity, those who had forgiven jumped higher than those who had not. Here's what researchers concluded: "A state of unforgiveness is like carrying a heavy burden—a burden that victims bring with them when they navigate the physical world. Forgiveness can 'lighten' this burden." They also said, "Forgivers perceive a less daunting world and perform better on challenging physical tasks."

Forgiveness is shown to increase the health of one's heart and overall cardiovascular system, while anger, which is typically present in the absence of forgiveness, can make the heart weaker.[4] The poison of anger can cause the heart to become less efficient in pumping and circulating blood, which ultimately means the rest of the body gets less oxygen. Less oxygen to the rest of the body can lower a person's immune system and cause fatigue.

In another study, 6,500 people responded to the question, "Would you say this is true or false: I've held grudges against people for years?"[5] Those who reported holding grudges had higher rates of stomach ulcers, back problems, chronic pain, headaches, and higher blood pressure than those who did not. This is why quick-witted Anne Lamott wisely says, "Not forgiving is like drinking rat poison and then waiting for the rat to die."[6] Grudges are toxic to those who harbor them.

Although forgiveness does *not* require forgetting, research shows that a by-product of forgiveness *is* forgetting.[7] In other words, forgiveness allows you to move away from painful events. Not having them at the forefront of your consciousness allows you to focus instead on the beauty and goodness all around you.

No wonder God encourages us to "bear with each other and forgive one another if any of you has a grievance against someone. Forgive as the Lord forgave you" (Col. 3:13). God wants us to forgive because it is in his DNA, and he wants us to be like him. But he also asks us to forgive because he knows the emotional, physical, and spiritual consequences of not forgiving. In other words, God wants us to forgive so we can live. If we continue to allow the seeds of anger, bitterness, rage, and resentment to soil our hearts, they will reap disastrous consequences in our lives. God's tenderness and love for us moves him to command us to forgive.

We've now extensively covered the idea of forgiving your ex. I want to conclude this chapter by discussing forgiveness on two different levels—forgiving yourself and forgiving God.

Forgive Yourself

You may have transgressed an inner vow or value and caused an injury to yourself before, during, or after your breakup. In essence, you have become both the victim and the assailant. Because you believe you did something wrong, you are resentful and angry with yourself. You can't let the act go. You continue to beat yourself up for it, making self-forgiveness so important.

From the late 1200s through the 1300s, a Christian sect took self-punishment to the extreme. At certain times, they went on long sacred pilgrimages, shouted out their sins they were struggling with, got down on one knee, and lashed themselves using whips tipped with sharp pieces of iron. The more religious of the bunch lashed themselves to the point of tearing their own flesh, causing blood to run down their bodies. This is where we get the term *self-flagellation*, which basically means self-punishment.

The Flagellants loved God but certainly could have used a lesson or two in self-compassion and self-forgiveness. And they definitely needed instruction on what Jesus had accomplished for them on the cross.

I have met many Christians who quote dozens of verses on how God loves and forgives them but act as the Flagellants did. They don't use literal whips; rather, they say harsh and critical words to themselves or engage in self-destructive behaviors to punish themselves. They believe an unconscious lie that says if they can make themselves hurt or feel bad enough, that will make up for what they did. Of course, it only causes more damage in the long run.

Bria, a woman I met in church, loved God but couldn't forgive herself for causing her breakup. She and her ex had been married for ten years and had two kids, but he divorced her after finding out she had cheated on him when she went to a conference out of state.

The divorce turned her world upside down. A tsunami of grief flooded her with self-hatred and shame. In the initial aftermath of the breakup, she starved herself and engaged in sex with random strangers to punish herself for what she had done.

Of course none of this made any sense because self-hatred and self-punishment never do. They make things worse. Bria thought that by hurting herself she could make up for the damage she caused to her family, but her actions only entrenched the shame and propelled her into even more destructive actions. She desperately needed help. Thank God, she eventually received God's forgiveness and forgave herself.

You are forgiven. You don't have to punish yourself. C. S. Lewis wrote, "I think that if God forgives us we must forgive ourselves. Otherwise, it is almost like setting up ourselves as a higher tribunal than Him."[8] Think about it. When you punish yourself, you are declaring that what Jesus went through on the cross was not good enough. The faulty equation states, *Jesus + Punishing Yourself = Complete Forgiveness*. But of course, that is like saying $1 + 1 = 5$. It is just plain wrong.

I don't mean to add to your guilt or shame by correcting your theological math. I'm trying to keep you from harming yourself further. If you are having a difficult time forgiving yourself, then talk to God. According to 1 John 1:9, God is faithful, he will forgive you, and he will make you clean and whole again. Psalm 103:11–12 says, "For as high as the heavens are above the earth, so great is his love for those who fear him; as far as the east is from the west, so far has he removed our transgressions from us."

Let the truth of God's profound love for you and the depth of his forgiveness dwell deeply in your heart. Then, when his love fills every nook and cranny of your tender heart, you can drop that devilish whip and treat yourself the way God treats you.

Forgive God

Even *talking* about forgiving God always seems sacrilegious, doesn't it? But if we're honest, the notion is always bubbling directly under the surface. James White, author of *Grieving: Our Path Back to Peace*, writes, "In our moments of honest reflection, we may have to confess in reality we are angry with God. If He is in control (and He is) then the change in my life came from His hand. And I don't like this change. I'm angry, and yes, I'm angry with God."[9]

Admitting that we are angry with God is extremely hard. Some people believe God is so holy that directing anger toward him is unholy, disrespectful, and sinful. That sounds nice and religious, but it is just not true. God is not like a grumpy earthly father who, out of anger, harshly punishes his child because she pitched a tantrum. Unlike us, God gives us an enormous amount of freedom to speak to him honestly from our innermost being—to share the good, the bad, the beautiful, and the ugly.

Jeremiah, the emotional prophet, otherwise known as "the weeping prophet," knew this about God. He shared how he really felt about his perception that God betrayed him. In Jeremiah 20:7, he wrote, "You deceived me, LORD, and I was deceived; you overpowered me and prevailed." It is precisely because Jeremiah had faith in a patient and understanding God that he could share those intimate thoughts.

If in your hurt you blame your breakup and heartbreak on God, perhaps you need to work through the steps of the REACH model of forgiveness discussed earlier. Why live with a fractured relationship with the One who created you and loves you, and who is in your corner passionately wanting you to experience a peaceful, uncomplicated relationship with him? "It's complicated," a phrase often written on Facebook walls, should not have to refer to our relationship with God.

Even though we may feel at times that God has betrayed us, the truth is we need to be the ones who ask for forgiveness. It is most likely we perceive God as responsible for our misery because of our mind-sets. But I am getting ahead of myself. In part IV, we will explore how our beliefs about God can cause us more suffering.

Just as a parent would want to validate his or her child's feelings when a cherished doll's head falls off, God probably wants to validate our feelings when we are betrayed. Whether or not forgiving him is warranted, God understands our limited perspective and validates our real experiences. God knows our brains aren't capable of understanding the wonders and mysteries of the universe as they relate to our lives. Even Job, another master griever, questioner, and complainer, who lost more than I could ever imagine, shouted, "How great is God—beyond our understanding!" (Job 36:26).

Forgiving your ex, yourself, and God can be among the most challenging—and rewarding—decisions you can make. God will never ask you to attempt such Olympic-sized feats by yourself. Where the finger of God points, the hand of God will provide. You can rest assured that God will supply you with the grace and power to forgive, for your freedom and his glory.

CHAPTER 15

Serve, Don't Swerve

God is a God of motion, of movement,
of mission. Or, as it is popular nowadays
to say, "two-thirds of the word God is go."
—LEONARD SWEET, *So Beautiful*

The night before a heavy-hearted Jesus was going to die, he told and showed his disciples what was important. Typically, people who know they are going to die share their hearts with those they dearly love—making sure everything they need to say actually gets said. That is exactly what Jesus did.

Jesus could have emphasized his disciples' need to understand deep theology and delved into the mysteries of the Trinity, the nuances of pneumatology, or the secrets of eschatology. But instead, Jesus emphasized and demonstrated to his disciples how to become sacrificial, servant followers. John 13:4–5 says, Jesus "got up from the meal, took off his outer clothing, and wrapped a towel around his waist. After that, he poured water into a basin and began to wash his disciples' feet, drying them with the towel that was wrapped around him."

The story of Jesus washing the disciples' feet is an incredible example of the humility and life of service he modeled for us. The perfect and holy God of the universe came down from heaven, enrobed himself in flesh as the God/man Jesus Christ, and began to do the inconceivable. The day before he was to suffer immeasurably, Jesus Christ, the incarnate God, chose to wash the crusty, smelly feet of sinful men. By this act, he extended extravagant grace to these men, including the rash, impulsive Peter, and Judas, the man who would betray him a day later. Jesus also did the inconceivable from a cultural perspective. In the Jewish culture, it was typically the poor Gentile slave who stooped down that low and washed the feet of the host and his guests. Nonetheless, Jesus defied cultural norms, and chose to humbly serve and give us an example to follow. (Jesus's greatest example of servanthood was going to the cross for the sake of the world.)

Grieving heartbreak in a healthy manner is a journey that does not happen overnight. For a while, you might feel as if you are living in a haunted house. You go through your days, doing what you need to do to survive and thrive, and all of a sudden the ghosts of intrusive memories pop up at unexpected times. And they bring along ghastly pain, sadness, anger, or misery that throw you into a tailspin. To grieve well you will need to learn how to pick up your cross, follow Jesus, and serve others in the midst of these hauntings.

Take Up Your Cross and Follow Him

We are all called to be humble followers of Christ who choose, despite circumstances, to serve others and not swerve around them. In other words, we are called to a head and heart collision into the lives of other people, not to swerve or avoid them just because we are experiencing pain.

I understand if you want a season of *being* rather than *doing*. You certainly have a right to allow sufficient time to deal with the immediate aftermath of the breakup. Someone who was just sideswiped in a terrible automobile accident and left with severe whiplash usually doesn't go to work the next day. Only you can hear the Father's voice and decide how much time you need to take off.

At some point, though, you must take up your cross, surrender your broken heart to Jesus, and live out your core mission. Keep in mind that being ready doesn't mean being healed or pain free; it doesn't mean you no longer feel as if you're living in a haunted house. It just means being ready to engage in the mission God has for you. It is like a dancer with a sore foot pressing on through the pain and going onstage determined to give a breathtaking and passionate performance or like a soldier with a high fever refusing to give in and standing with his brothers-in-arms on the battlefield. Like them you must be determined not to let anything come between you and your God-given calling.

The Blessedness of Serving

The Purpose Driven Life has sold more than thirty million copies and has been one of the most popular Christian books of the last few decades for a reason. Finding one's purpose and fulfilling it in the world is a transformative experience. According to Acts 20:35, Jesus wisely said, "It is more blessed to give than to receive." When you use the gifts God has given you to serve others, your sense of purpose and meaning bubble up to the surface, giving you a profound joy that not only buffers you against the overwhelming feelings of grief, but over time, contribute to the mending of your heart.

Many research studies have shown that embracing your life's purpose actually contributes to reducing anxiety, depression, and loneliness, and can actually increase your life expectancy.[1] Getting your mind off your pain and onto God's grand purpose for your life creates resiliency to the trauma of your breakup. In

Luke 6:38, Jesus says, "Give, and it will be given to you. A good measure, pressed down, shaken together and running over, will be poured into your lap."

The Christian life is about *inspiration* that leads to *perspiration* in a context of *conspiration* or there will be *expiration*. It is not enough to merely be inspired by the Bible or sermons from pastors and other eloquent teachers. We are called to perspire— to undertake a mission, to sweat out and exude the love of Christ through the unique gifts and personalities God has given us. But we are to do this as a conspiration, a joint effort with other wounded, lovesick warriors who are also on a mission. If we reach a point where we are no longer inspired missional members of the body of Christ in God's service to the world, part of our soul will shrivel up and die. God never meant for us to live purposelessly, without mission and movement, isolated and alone.

When you love and serve others as you were designed to do, healing from grief becomes a natural by-product. Healing is the result of obeying God, despite your pain, and choosing to steadfastly live out the adventure you were created for. Your inner flame of purpose and passion grows exponentially when you look outside yourself and give to others. Serving others leaves you with a feeling of vibrancy and joy. It reminds you that your life is much bigger than your heartbreak. You start to realize that although one chapter has come to an end, there are other chapters yet to be lived.

Go for It!

If you have been grieving, feeling bogged down, and isolating yourself—refusing to focus on others—open your heart to the practice and sacred discipline of serving others. You are as unique as the flowers in a field. Romans 12:6 says, "We have different gifts, according to the grace given to each of us." First Peter 4:10 says, "Each of you should use whatever gift you have received to serve others, as faithful stewards of God's grace in its various forms." Jesus never meant for you to sit passively on a couch, bitter and broken, living vicariously through characters in the pixel fantasylands of television and movies. He created you to be an active adventurer. Spiritual gifts are in your DNA. The Creator of the universe gave them to you to accomplish a mission of love, service, and grace to others. The key is not losing that big picture during your season of heartbreak.

As Jesus captivates your hurting heart and you are filled with God's presence, and as you enjoy the fellowship and healing balm of community, the Holy Spirit will woo you to venture outward. As you move outward, the Holy Spirit will lead you to love, connect, and live the missionary life God calls all people to live, experiencing love-filled stories along the way.

At the end of our difficult but rewarding journey on earth, one of the most blessed things would be to hear God lovingly say, "Well done, good and faithful servant" (Matt. 25:21). Don't let any person or circumstance keep you from that magnificent destiny!

PART IV

Grieving Ponderings

The word ponderings *can mean "weighty reflections." As important as it is to understand your grieving process and find pathways and practices to help you on your journey to a healed heart, it is also important to reflect deeply on broader issues surrounding grief. My intention for including these ponderings is to help you think through relevant topics in new ways. I desire not only to help you grieve well but also to help you confidently guide and support others experiencing loss and grief, whom you will eventually encounter. This last section is filled with philosophical and theological ponderings about empathic listening, culture, God, suffering, and hope.*

Although these next two chapters are important for your overall grieving process, I understand if they might be too heady, especially if your breakup was very recent. You might need to focus on fostering relationships and engaging in healing practices for a while before you start immersing yourself in deep cultural and theological reflection. That is okay. Take your time, and revisit these chapters when you are ready.

CHAPTER 16

In Need of Story Catchers

Listening is a magnetic and strange thing,
a creative force. The friends who listen to us are
the ones we move toward. When we are listened to,
it creates us, makes us unfold and expand.
—BRENDA UELAND, *Ladies' Home Journal*, 1941

James 1:19 encourages us to "be quick to listen, slow to speak," instead of being quick to speak and slow to listen, which seems to be far more common. Truth be told, there are times when I am just as guilty. I am a pastor and a counselor, but at times I zone out when a person is sharing his or her heart with me. I catch myself drifting, begin to listen authentically, and then drift again a short time later. Despite its difficulty, I am convinced that one of the most practical and powerful ways people can love heartbroken people like you is by listening—becoming what I call story catchers.

Story Catchers

Story catchers practice deep, empathic, compassionate listening. They are intentional about catching the stories of others, about listening lovingly to the blessings and blunders of those they encounter. Story catchers embody acceptance, compassion, and grace. Heartfelt story catching communicates messages such as "You are loved," "You are worth it," "You are respected," and "You are valued."

One of the story catcher's favorite life verses might be 1 Peter 3:8: "Finally, all of you, be like-minded, be sympathetic, love one another, be compassionate and humble." Story catchers believe like-mindedness, sympathy, compassion, and humility are the route to deep, intimate relationships. They are serious about the biblical mandate to tune in to the emotional and spiritual frequency of others (like-minded), to notice the suffering that others are experiencing and enter into their pain (sympathy) with tenderheartedness (compassion), and by acknowledging another person's inherent worth as a fellow journeyer who needs the grace of God as much as they do (humility).

Carl Rogers, a famous and influential psychologist, has this inspiring definition of empathic listening: "It means entering the private perceptual world of the other and becoming thoroughly at home in it. It involves being sensitive, moment by moment, to the changing felt meanings which flow in this other person, to the fear or rage or tenderness or confusion or whatever he or she is experiencing. It means temporarily living in the other's life, moving about in it delicately without making judgments."[1]

The above definition reminds me of the television show *Hoarders*. I will never forget an episode that featured a hoarding therapist named Cory, who decided to sleep inside a house packed to the rafters with clothes and garbage. Insects and rodents scurried over the heaps. And the home did not have heat. Cory wanted to experience what the hoarder experienced as a way of truly entering and understanding her world. He certainly ended up with a frightening taste of what it was like to live as she did (spoiler alert, he didn't get a good night's sleep).

Cory's decision to enter into the multisensory experience of someone who was hurting is what I think the Bible and Carl Rogers were getting at. Story catchers proactively make a pact to cherish deep emotional, spiritual, and physical contact with those they encounter. They are willing to enter people's homes, no matter how messy, dark, or scary. Like Cory, they might feel nervous and uncomfortable at times, but they do the work courageously, knowing that through story catching they can love the hell out of people. *Hell*, in this case, signifies those things that torment or weigh heavily on hurting and "dis-eased" people.

Story catchers do not believe depth of connection can be found on the surface of people's thoughts, but in the place where emotions reside—where "deep calls to deep" (Ps. 42:7). They recognize that behind emotions—such as fear, sadness, loneliness, hurt, and shame—linger relational questions and longings, such as,

> Will you listen to me?
>
> Will you love me?
>
> Will you comfort me?
>
> Will you be there for me?
>
> Will you be proud of me?
>
> Will you hold me?

Emotions become a window through which story catchers are able to peer to access deeper parts of people's hearts and stories. By listening to the stories and accessing and acknowledging the deeper emotions and longings, story catchers often leave hurting people feeling profoundly understood. Those who experience a story catcher's ministry say they feel lighter and freer, and more connected to God, self, and others.

Shanna's Story

Let's look at a story catcher in action. Shanna and Steve, who were friends and employees at a department store, were hanging out in the break room during lunch one day. Steve saw that Shanna was a little out of sorts and asked her what was going on.

"I don't know what's wrong with me," she said. "I broke up with my boyfriend, and I have been feeling really sad lately."

Steve moved into story-catching mode and began to pray a simple silent prayer. "God, help me catch her story." He set his iPhone to silent, turned his body toward her, and made appropriate (non-creepy) eye contact with her. He homed in on her sadness and knew intuitively that she might be asking, on an unconscious level, for someone to listen and provide some level of comfort.

"This sounds like a really difficult time for you," he said. "Do you want to talk about it?"

She was hesitant at first, but sensed Steve was sincere, so she began to share her story.

He listened intently, imagining what it must be like to be in her situation and felt honored that she would share her story with him. When they had to get back to work, he took a risk and asked if he could say a short prayer for her.

When he prayed, she was deeply moved and God probably smiled.

Story catching is taking time out of one's schedule to listen to another person who is in distress (or in joy, for that matter).

Hannah's Grief

First Samuel includes the story of Elkanah and his two wives, Hannah and Peninnah: "Peninnah had children, but Hannah had none" (1 Sam. 1:2). In Hannah's culture, having children—being "fruitful" (Gen. 1:28)—was a sign of blessing and favor from God. But because Hannah was unable to bear a child, some people would have thought her cursed. To add to Hannah's grief, Peninnah was "provoking her in order to irritate her," so much so that Hannah "wept and would not eat"; what is worse, "this went on year after year" (1 Sam. 1:6–7). If Peninnah had done that to some of the women I know, she would have gotten knocked out cold, but that was not Hannah's style. Hannah suffered the shame and disgrace of barrenness in silence.

Hannah was desperate and needed an empathic story catcher. She needed her husband Elkanah, the most important person in her universe, to validate her experience and to empathize with her suffering, shame, and sorrow. Here is what Elkanah, the man of God, said to Hannah while she was grieving: "Hannah, why are you weeping? Why don't you eat? Why are you downhearted? Don't I mean more to you than ten sons?" (v. 8).

Elkanah could have used a few lessons on relational intelligence and the sacred art of empathic listening. He had spent many years with his wife and still didn't have a clue about the depths of her grief. He might as well have said, "Hey, babe, why are you so upset about what you don't have? Don't feel that way. You've got me." Epic failure.

He was clueless, but they didn't have marriage seminars or access to classic books like *Men Are from Mars, Women Are from Venus* back then.

During your season of heartbreak, have you experienced something similar to what Hannah endured? Perhaps you have tried to share your story and instead of finding someone who was empathic and compassionate, people shut you down or minimized your pain, making you feel invalidated. Maybe your friends or family were more subtle in the way they brushed you off, advising you to read your Bible or to get something to eat.

A recent study looking at 217 people who recently went through a breakup showed that those who experienced support from friends and loved ones experienced less distress, such as anxiety, depression, loneliness, and hurt.[2] The study also showed that "social constraints are associated with psychological distress and are likely to impact recovery from a breakup."[3] In other words, when those who were hurting after a breakup went to talk about their pain with friends and loved ones, and those they went to instantly changed the subject, minimized or trivialized their pain, and nonchalantly told them not to worry about it, the heartbroken experienced more suffering and took longer to recover and heal from the breakup.

A few months ago I met a woman who was going through a breakup. She knew exactly how it felt to have her feelings minimized.

"I feel so isolated and alone," she said. "I try to talk to people about my breakup and the anguish I am experiencing, but they tell me, 'Cheer up, sister, God has a plan.' Or someone approaches me, and I start to feel excited because they appear genuinely interested, but they quickly flip it around and make it all about them."

If you haven't been heard during your grief, you are not alone. Unfortunately, story catchers are rare, especially in our culture, for several reasons.

Anti-Gravity

We live in an anti-gravity culture. The prefix *anti-* means "against," and *gravity* comes from the Latin word *gravitas*, which means "heavy or weighty." In other words, we live in a culture that is against dealing with the weightier matters of the heart, such as grief, loss, fear, shame, pain, and other heavy experiences. We would much rather swim in the shallow waters than in the depths of each other's darker, more negative emotional experiences.

Our society has always squelched natural and healthy expressions of emotion with anti-gravity statements like these:

Don't cry.

Are you sad? This pill will help you smile again.

Suck it up.

Don't be a sissy.

Don't show weakness.

Hey, be a man.

Don't be so emotional.

Aren't you over him yet?

Put on your big-girl panties and deal with it.

Sure, we might ask one another how we are doing, on a regular basis, but seldom is it a real inquiry. Usually it's merely a polite social greeting, and it's followed by the typical programmed response, "Good, thanks."

Shallow responses from people who mean well often contain hidden messages like, "Snap out of it!" or "Forget the pain, and put a smile on your face." They are either saying that you aren't supposed to feel the way you feel, or they simply don't have time or empathy to enter your experience. They don't realize you need a listening ear and truth that comes from a compassionate heart.

Authentic and active listening can be hard for all of us. While there can be many reasons for that, I want to explore a few obstacles to becoming story catchers: our addiction to perfection, being tethered to technology, and blazing busyness.

Addiction to Perfection

Did you know that Americans spend roughly $77 billion a year on the perfect landscape?[4] I feel the need to repeat that, just to let it sink in. Americans spend $77 billion a year to have finely shaped, vibrant green grass and bushes on their properties. Perfect landscapes symbolize their fetish for perfection.

Did you know that with modern technology we can screen for genetic illnesses, choose a male or female embryo, and identify the healthiest embryo in the lot—all to obtain the "perfect child"?

Our culture elevates strong, sexy, vibrant, and plastic over weak, average, weary, and wrinkled. Men and women, many of whom we watch on our favorite television programs or see in the movies, spend billions of dollars a year on cosmetic surgeries to get perfect bodies.

We listen to music that has been so produced and polished that it is impossible to perform some songs live, which is why so many well-known artists get caught lip-syncing their way through "live" performances.

We are immersed in a culture that is addicted to perfection, and that pursuit can have devastating and grave consequences. Ted Steinberg, a well-known historian, points out the negative consequences of what would seem like a benign addiction to the perfect lawn:

> Using a gas-powered leaf blower for half an hour creates as many polluting hydrocarbon emissions as driving a car seventy-seven hundred miles at a speed of thirty miles per hour. Approximately seven million birds die each year because of lawn-care pesticides. In the process of refueling their lawn mowers, leaf blowers, and other garden equipment, Americans spill about seventeen million gallons of gasoline every summer, or about 50 percent more oil than marred the Alaskan coast during the notorious Exxon *Valdez* disaster.[5]

Environmental disasters, eating disorders, cosmetic surgeries, addictions, and an aversion to natural human emotions, such as sadness and fear, are some of the many consequences that have their roots in a perfectionistic culture. This clinging to the ideal notion of perfection keeps people from entering into their own and other people's painful stories.

Hidden within the word *perfectionism*, at least phonetically, is the word *shun*, which is a constant reminder of the unfortunate consequence of trying to be perfect. I like to think of *perfectionism* as *perfect*-shun-*ism*.

When we shun somebody, we keep away from, hide from, or avoid that person. We, who are affected by perfect*shun*ism tend to avoid or shun anything that appears to be broken, incomplete, raw, and imperfect. Perfect*shun*ism invariably keeps us from listening to the brokenness within ourselves and others, and it keeps others from engaging with and listening to us. It stops us from knowing each other and ourselves, intimately.

Perfect*shun*ism causes us to fear the raw, unrefined inner experience and to shun what our souls are really crying out for. So we mask our imperfect pain with excessive activity, noise, programs, addictions, and the like. We may fear the brokenness of others as well. If we run away from our own pain, shame, and brokenness, we will most likely run away from broken people who come to us in their time of need and desperation.

Perfect*shun*ism also causes us to look like something we are not, which puts a barrier between who we really are and other people. Since we will never be perfect, our attempts at showing people our perfection hides our inner selves from them. People then see and experience our personas, not the real us. If we relate to people and God as we think we should (like an actor), then we keep others from listening and encountering the real us.

Tethered to Technology

We have become so addicted to technology that we have developed a phenomenon called phantom vibration syndrome (PVS).

PVS occurs when we are so hypervigilant that we hurriedly check our cell phones because we felt the phone vibrate or thought we heard it ring, but, in reality, nobody texted, sent a Facebook message, or called us. It was all in our anxious imagination. PVS is not the only cost to us for being saturated in technology and social media.

Although Facebook, Twitter, Instagram, Pinterest, Google+, and the like can be great ways to connect with others, they cannot adequately provide the type of intimacy and face-to-face presence that people crave. Social networking, and technology in general, does provide some benefits though. It can be a blessing when you are having a difficult night and need an encouraging word. But as great as such an experience is, it is not enough. Shane Hipps writes, "It's a bit like cotton candy: It goes down easy and satiates our immediate hunger, but it doesn't provide much in the way of sustainable nutrition."[6]

One of the major problems with technology is that, as it replaces face-to-face encounters, there are fewer opportunities to practice deep, empathic, and compassionate listening. Since listening is a skill that is developed over time, we face a use-it-or-lose-it situation. I can't help but wonder if younger generations are ever going to develop the skill of listening. If nobody ever models it for them, they will never have the opportunity to learn it. Just as we are in danger of losing valuable artisans because of increasing technology, so we are in danger of losing skilled story catchers.

Busyness

Have you ever felt the need to connect with someone, but everybody seemed too busy? Why even bother, right? Your intuition was probably correct. Making time to listen to one another doesn't happen easily in our hustle-and-bustle culture, in which, whether we realize it or not, most of us have ADHD. We are just way too busy with work, church, small groups, meals, service projects, emails and texts, pop-up media messages, favorite television shows, hobbies, and so on, and so on.

Staying so busy is affecting us in such negative ways that there is now a term for it: *hurry sickness*. Officially, the term is defined as "a modern malady caused by constant rushing. A compulsion to do everything quickly, or a chronic feeling of being short of time, attributed to the fast pace of modern life, which causes symptoms such as anxiety and insomnia."[7] We are simply not designed for the fast and frenetic pace at which we are moving and it is taking a toll on us. Not only is there an epidemic of insomnia, ulcers, and anxiety disorders but busyness is also affecting our relationships. When afflicted with hurry sickness, giving people our undivided attention is next to impossible.

I hope you're beginning to gain some empathy for those who are unable to be wholly present and listen to you during your season of heartbreak. It is not that people don't care about you. They just live at such a fast pace that they don't believe they have time to be a story catcher. In truth, perfectionism, technology, and busyness are realities we all have to contend with in our present culture. I am thankful though, that because of God's Spirit and through a disciplined intention, we don't have to let them get the best of us.

Going Against the Grain

As story catchers, we don't have to conform to our culture. We don't have to let obstacles get in the way of compassionately listening to the stories of others, as well as listening to our own during times of silence and solitude. It will not be easy, but we can choose to contend for the biblical mandate to embody like-mindedness, sympathy, compassion, and humility, wherever we go.

Practically, we can go against the grain by choosing not to shun but to honor others' and our own messy and imperfect emotional and spiritual experiences. We can lean in intentionally and listen to pain and suffering wherever it is found. Story catchers throw perfect*shun*ism out the window and vow to encounter both the horrid and the holy gracefully, within and without, until the day we breathe our last breath.

We can take our story-catching cues from Jesus. Being fearless, Jesus was the epitome of a story catcher. He did not shun his own difficult emotional experiences but expressed his feelings freely (Mark 14:34; John 11:35), and he dove deep into the pain and shame of others (John 4:1–26; 8:1–11).

We don't need to bear false witness about our experiences, nor do we need to encourage others to do so. We can give ourselves and others permission to be messy and imperfect, because we know that God loves all of us just as we are. Of course, God doesn't leave us where we are but gently guides us into greater measures of abundant living. *Abundant living* is code for the degree to which we are able to love and be loved by God, others, and ourselves.

Additionally, we can go against the grain of our technologically addicted culture and not let social networking become our sole means of connection. That is not to demonize technology and social media. I am sure Jesus would be tweeting, texting, and tagging away if he were walking the earth today. We just don't want to become relationally anemic by excluding the most important aspect of connection—heart-to-heart, face-to-face encounters with other people.

In practice, prioritizing relationships will mean intentionally choosing people over pixels. One practice for helping yourself follow through might be to write yourself a note about engaging in the fine art of listening and to attach it to your refrigerator at home or to your desk at work. You could write, "How many times this week have I been face-to-face with others catching their stories?" or "How many times this week have I been face-to-face with others letting them catch my stories?" Another practice might be to meet a friend for coffee at the same time and place every Saturday morning, and to take a sabbatical from your devices while you're there. Silence your cell phone and place it face down. Forget about your email or texts and simply focus on the person across from you.

Lastly, we have to keep ourselves from getting sucked into the dizziness of busyness. We do this by saying no more often— to our boss, our church, and that new epic television series that demand more time from us. Saying no to things that are not a priority is saying yes to what we value most: God and the people he has placed in our lives. Story catchers make it their business to keep busyness at bay so they can offer their presence to God and to others.

The Call

Because of your own suffering, you understand the need for story catchers. I pray that after you experience the healing effects of story catchers in your life, you will avoid cultural obstacles and heed the call to become a story catcher yourself for relationship-starved people. There is a world full of people who are longing to be heard and craving an opportunity to tell their stories to someone who cares. Remember, the word *ear* is in the word *heart* to remind us that the fastest way to one's heart is through listening to them.

CHAPTER 17

A Theology of Suffering

*As I took up life as a minister, I tried to understand why so
many people resisted and rejected God. I soon realized that
perhaps the main reason was affliction and suffering.*
—Timothy Keller, *Walking with God Through Pain and Suffering*

In the movie *Serendipity*, Sara goes on a quest to find a man
she met many years ago, thinking he might be her only chance
at true love. She travels back to New York with her best friend,
Eve, to search for him. They end up in a pastry shop that shares
the name of the movie. There Eve tries to console Sara when
their quest falls short.

"Sara, you know it's a wonderful thought—the idea that all
of life, that every single event is all part of some master plan
designed to lead us to our universal soul mate," she says.
"If that's really true, then what's the point of living or making decisions? Why should we even get out of bed in the
morning?"

"For the cake?" Sara offers.

"No, not the cake. It's so that you make mistakes—mistakes like this trip. And if you're smart enough, you learn
from your mistakes. You figure it out. You think. You realize

that life isn't some elaborate stage play with directions for the actors. Life's a mess, Sara. It's chaos personified."[1]

In our modern culture, many people view life similarly to the way Eve does. For them, there is no plan, ultimate purpose, or God at work in the world or in their lives. There is only random selection, evolution, and the by-product of soulless human beings comprised of trillions of living cells and billions of neurons making choices. From such a perspective, there is no quagmire (complex or muddy situation) to figure out. Suffering should occur in a purposeless universe. To experience a heartbreak, for example, is normal and to be expected in a world ruled by chaos and chance (although ironically these same people complain when they experience it, as if it *should* have been another way).

A Christian Quagmire

The theological quagmire surrounding evil and suffering exists only for Christians, or those who believe in a benevolent deity. Only we are forced to wrestle with why an all-powerful, all-loving sovereign God—who, according to the Bible, is in control of everything—allows us to experience evil and suffering. If there is no God, there is no quagmire. But because we believe there is a God, we wrestle through the quagmire. What you believe about God in the midst of your excruciating heartbreak will cause you either to flourish or to flounder.

Meeting people who have turned away from God because they have suffered horrific traumas, devastating losses, heartbreaks, and the like revs my engine and triggers my holy discontent. I have encountered many heartbroken Christians who, after a devastating breakup, have said something to the effect of, "Why did God break my heart like this? God must be cruel. He can't be trusted." Instead of turning to a loving God who wants to enter into their suffering with them, they withdraw from God because they believed he intentionally planned and orchestrated the breakup.

Kimberley Kennedy, who authored the book, *Left at the Altar*, wrote about her devastating heartbreak after the man she was going to spend the rest of her life with literally left her at the altar. She wrote the following about her feelings toward God after her breakup:

> There were actually two endeavors I did enjoy. The first was blaming, hating, and yelling at God. I was so angry at him for allowing this terrible thing to happen and destroy my life. The only Bible verse that made any sense to me at all was the one where Jesus is on the cross, and he says, "My God, my God, why have you forsaken me?" (Matt. 27:46). I felt that God had totally abandoned me when he knew better than anybody that I deserved to have something good happen. In my mind, I had been a good person, a faithful churchgoer; God should have intervened and made Lew marry me.[2]

Although Kimberley would later experience God's mercy in beautiful and surprising ways, much of her initial thinking and feelings toward God could have been different. Unfortunately, Kimberley and others turn away from God in the midst of loss, in large part, because they do not have an adequate theology of suffering. They do not have a foundational theology that helps them make sense of God's role in their suffering. And the little or faulty theology they do have leads them astray, so that they blame God and become utterly lost in heartbreak and despair.

Like Kimberley, some people can eventually take hold of God's grace and get out of their dark night of the soul. Others gradually stop praying. Then they stop going to church. Finally, they may even walk away from the faith entirely. If they remain in the faith, they often do so from a distance. Unfortunately, that distance robs them of the very things that would help them through their heartbreak—restorative prayer and intimacy with God.

Evil and Suffering Defined

When people think about the concept of evil, they typically think of heinous and morally reprehensible acts like murder, rape, and genocide. While all of these acts are evil, the biblical concept of evil is much broader. Simply put, evil is anything contrary to the will of God, such as thoughts (Gen. 6:5), deeds (Prov. 5:22), desires (Rom. 6:12), spirits (Mark 3:11), etc. Suffering is an inner cognitive/emotional experience in reaction to such things. But suffering can also come about from non-evil events. For example, a child who is told to go to bed early by his parents may experience suffering, but the event of going to bed early is not necessarily an evil act. Where there is evil, suffering is usually not far behind; however, where there is suffering, evil is not always present.

Evil, loss, and suffering are common to all people in all places and socioeconomic statuses. No one can escape their effects, no matter how rich or poor they are or where they live on the earth. If you don't have an adequate understanding, the weight of evil, loss, and suffering can crush you. Your theology can either deepen your suffering or bring deep consolation during your season of heartbreak. It is time to rethink our theology of suffering. It is time for a new, updated map based on prayerful reflection and Scripture.

I believe we "see only a reflection as in a mirror" and "know in part" (1 Cor. 13:12) when it comes to truth, but when it comes to understanding the mysteries of free will, suffering, and God's sovereignty, our mirror is a bit more foggy, increasing the difficulty of making out an accurate reflection. The remainder of this chapter offers some ponderings which, although they do not solve the problem of evil, build a solid foundation on which to ground a theology of suffering. My hope is that it not only will get you through your current season of heartbreak but also will help guide you throughout the rest of your life journey where losses of various kinds are inevitable. Let's glean some insights from the parable of the wheat and the tares.

The Parable of the Wheat and the Tares

The gospel of Matthew was written to a community experiencing trauma. The people were dealing with identity concerns, religious pluralism, infighting, the government's abuse of power, social and economic injustice, and many other difficult issues. Like us, the community wrestled with how a great God could allow good and evil to exist simultaneously in and around the lives of believers. In Matthew, Jesus addresses the community's inner ache, curiosity, and questions:

> Jesus told them another parable: "The kingdom of heaven is like a man who sowed good seed in his field. But while everyone was sleeping, his enemy came and sowed weeds among the wheat, and went away. When the wheat sprouted and formed heads, then the weeds also appeared.
>
> "The owner's servants came to him and said, 'Sir, didn't you sow good seed in your field? Where then did the weeds come from?'
>
> "'An enemy did this,' he replied.
>
> "The servants asked him, 'Do you want us to go and pull them up?'
>
> "'No,' he answered, 'because while you are pulling the weeds, you may uproot the wheat with them. Let both grow together until the harvest. At that time I will tell the harvesters: First collect the weeds and tie them in bundles to be burned; then gather the wheat and bring it into my barn.'" (Matt. 13:24–30)

It's Okay to Cry Out

Notice the honesty and congruence of the servant in verse 27: "Sir, didn't you sow good seed in your field? Where then did the weeds come from?" The servant was confused about the weeds, as you may be confused in the midst of your heartbreak. The weeds, which can be synonymous for evil or painful experiences, created confusion for the servant, just as they do for us today, causing us to suffer. Our confusion ruptures our sense of security and trust, and stings our souls. It moves us to wonder what God is doing. That is a normal reaction. Even Jesus cried out in agony in Mark 15:34: "My God, my God, why have you forsaken me?"

As Christians, we cry out in protest to God because we have genuine faith. Questioning God when you are struggling to find answers in the midst of your pain is not sinful. Max Lucado writes, "It is better to shake a fist at God than to turn your back on him."[3] Asking God questions is a normal and holy act precisely because you lack genuine understanding and believe he knows the answers. Wrestling with God allows for new revelations concerning our existence. I am always more concerned for the people who stop questioning God and become cold and calloused toward him.

The Real Origin of Evil

Just as the servants in the parable were curious as to where the harmful weeds came from, we are curious as to where the evil and hardship in our lives come from. After a painful breakup, it is normal to want to make sense of what happened. The brain demands coherence because if it doesn't understand how you have come to hurt so deeply then it is possible it could happen in the future. Some blame the ex-partner. Others blame themselves.

Still others point the finger at God, perceiving that if God is in control of all things, and God is loving, then he must have caused their pain. We turn again to the parable for some insights into possible causes of our suffering.

The Enemy

The owner of the field knew the origin of the evil weeds, for he said, in verse 28, "An enemy did this." The servant knew that the owner was not the originator, creator, or cause of the evil that happened to him, just as God is not the originator, creator, or cause of the evil that happens to us. Thomas Long writes, "It should first be heard as the powerful good news that it is. Evil is God's enemy. Not God's instrument, not God's counterpart, not something about which God is indifferent. Evil is God's enemy, period."[4]

God isn't joyfully working behind the scenes, orchestrating crippling breakups and tragic divorces. There are other dynamics at play when bad things happen to good people such as satanic or adversarial forces, and people's free-will choices.

In our modern era, Satan tends to be something relegated to horror movies and TV shows but the Bible is very clear: Satan, literally meaning *adversary* in Hebrew, does exist.[5] According to 1 Peter 5:8, the enemy "prowls around like a roaring lion looking for someone to devour." Richard Beck, author of *Reviving Old Scratch: Demons and the Devil for Doubters and the Disenchanted*, defines Satan as "that which is *adversarial to the kingdom of God*."[6] He goes on to write that "while Christians might disagree about the exact nature of the forces arrayed against the kingdom, we recognize these forces as real and active in the world, forces that need to be fought and resisted."[7]

Satan, in whatever force, form, or guise he exists, should be taken seriously. Satan is witty, scheming, and plotting (2 Cor. 2:11), tempts people (Matt. 4:1; 1 Cor. 7:5), and tries to thwart the work of God in people's lives (1 Thess. 2:18). The enemy, a true mastermind of heartbreak, is prowling around, looking for relationships to devour. Satan, who is adversarial to loving connection in the world, works behind the scenes to encourage discord and disconnection. He delights in the aftermath of love destroyed, especially when it results in people's doubts in the goodness of God.

Free Will

We can't blame everything on Satan . . . or God. Much of the evil and suffering in the world is due to the free-will choices of those who said no to God and yes to their own selfish desires. For example, my client Barbara was devastated and heartbroken when her fiancé, Vincent, left her for another woman after a two-year affair. I don't believe God orchestrated Vincent's affair or made him leave Barbara for the other woman. Vincent made a willful choice to sin and betray Barbara and break her heart. I had a friend named Martin who was blindsided and crushed by his wife Andrea's request that he give her a divorce so she could follow her dreams and become an actress. I don't believe God caused, motivated, or inspired Andrea to leave Martin in order to pursue fame and fortune. We should not credit God for people's sinful and selfish choices.

While satanic influence and other people's choices may be contributing factors, we also need to be courageous enough to ask ourselves how our own choices have led to the breakup. There are times when we are our own worst enemy. We are prone to planting weeds in the garden of our hearts and lives, sabotaging God's seeds of faith, hope, and love. In all my years of working with heartbroken clients and congregants, I have found that asking ourselves how we might have contributed to our suffering is one of the most difficult questions to consider. It is much easier to point the finger at an ex, God, or Satan, and blame them for everything.

It could take many months' work before a client is ready for such a difficult, introspective journey. It certainly took me a while before I could ask myself the hard questions. Eventually, I found enough strength and courage and prayed one of the most "dangerous" prayers a Christian can pray. The prayer is found in Psalm 139:23–24: "Search me, God, and know my heart; test [examine] me and know my anxious [troubled] thoughts. See if there is any offensive [ôtseb in Hebrew, which can mean "mental or emotional suffering"] way in me, and lead me in the way everlasting."[8]

After much prayer and introspection, God showed me areas of my heart that were not yet conformed to the image of Christ. I realized that I had made choices from a wounded and immature heart that contributed to the breakup with my ex. It was a humbling revelation. Instead of pointing all the fingers at my ex, I began to realize I had to point a few at myself; I had played a part too. The more aware I was of my own sinful motives and actions, the less I blamed her for what happened and the more my heart softened toward her.

The reality is that we have sin-filled crevices in our soul, and because of that, we don't always do the things we ought to, to ensure a successful relationship. Because we have pockets of selfishness, pride, lust, and greed, and, perhaps, deep wounds from past traumas, we unwittingly contribute to the breakup and our own heartbreak. If we know what the sin crevices are filled with, we can ask God to dig them out and fill them with his goodness, beauty, and truth. Asking the hard questions is not an exercise meant to condemn us or make us feel ashamed, but to help us be Christlike and succeed in relationships in the future.

God?

I tend to resonate with the owner in the parable. God is not the master designer of evil or devastating events. The servants knew the character of the owner because they asked, in Matthew 13:27, "Didn't you sow good seed in your field?" God, who is portrayed as the owner, is good (all the time) and he sows only good seed. Another metaphor, used in Luke 6:43, says, "No good tree bears bad fruit, nor does a bad tree bear good fruit." It is reasonable to assume that God, who is the all-good Tree of Life, would not produce bad fruit. And, finally, God offers us "living" (John 4:10) and fresh water. James 3:11 says, "Can both fresh water and salt water flow from the same spring?" God's water contains no impurities. He is good all the time, bears only good nutritious fruit, and is the purest and freshest water imaginable. God doesn't cause evil. God is love. While I believe only good can come from God, there is a slight caveat.

God's good sometimes feels painful. Think about a loving parent who takes his or her child to a stranger in a white coat and lets the stranger use a large drill to repair a cavity in the child's little mouth. Although a trip to the dentist can be scary and painful, the parent puts his or her child through the ordeal only because he or she loves the child. Similarly, there are events that God moves us toward that hurt but are not evil in nature; they are, ultimately, for our good and God's glory.

Did you cause your breakup? Did your ex cause it? Did you both contribute to its demise? Did insidious sin cause it to fall apart? Was Satan at work wreaking havoc on your relationship? Honestly, I have no idea. It could have been a mysterious interaction of many of the above dynamics. The only thing I know for sure is that God is good all the time and sows only good seed.

A theology of suffering must rely heavily on the goodness of God. A theology of suffering must also take into consideration that God's will is not the only will in town. We must allow for both the work of the enemy and the choices of others, as well as our own. This is why we pray, "Your kingdom come, your will be done, on earth as it is in heaven" (Matt. 6:10). It doesn't make sense to pray for God's kingdom to come and his will to be done if God's rule and reign is already everywhere and his will is always done on earth. Yet Jesus calls us to pray that way because both the enemy and humans have wills, and both can be contrary to God's good and gracious will.

Evil and Suffering Are Here to Stay

The servants in the parable of the wheat and the tares wondered what the owner was going to do about the weeds, which is similar to our wondering what God is going to do to take care of the weeds of evil in the world. The servants asked the owner, "Do you want us to go and pull them [weeds] up?" and got this answer: "No, . . . because while you are pulling the weeds, you may uproot the wheat with them" (Matt. 13:28–29). God doesn't pull out all of the evil in the world. He has other plans.

The owner may have wanted the servants to focus primarily on his goodness and his loving commands, rather than the weeds, which is what God wants us to do presently. The by-product of focusing on what God has called us to do would inevitably root out some of the evil, as Romans 12:21 reminds us, "Do not be overcome by evil, but overcome evil with good." A Christian's life lived well is one of the biggest deterrents of evil. The rest of the evil must be left to its ultimate obliteration by God, in God's timing.

For the time being, evil—the absence of good, or spaces and places where the kingdom of God is not yet ruling and reigning —is here to stay. And with evil comes suffering. Jesus said, "In this world you will have trouble [*thlipsis*]" (John 16:33). The Greek word *thlipsis* can mean trouble, distress, oppression, and tribulation.[9] Heartbreak and other tragedies will happen even to those of us who love God. It hurts, and it is unfair. But, dearly beloved, God is not reveling in your pain. Although evil exists and God is not the grand puppeteer of every detail of your life, that doesn't mean he is idle.

God Has a Plan

The owner of the field finally says to the servants, "Let both grow together until the harvest. At that time I will tell the harvesters: First collect the weeds and tie them in bundles to be burned; then gather the wheat and bring it into my barn" (Matt. 13:30).

There is hope. Just as the owner had a plan, so does God. God is not shocked and paralyzed with fear because of all the horrific evil and suffering in the world. He is not clueless, unable to figure out what to do next. God is sovereign. Not only did God become the answer to our sin and evil problem and show us the way of salvation in and through Jesus, God is presently in control, leading humanity to God's unfolding purposes. Just not in the way we think.

God demonstrates a profoundly different type of leadership than that demonstrated by powerful and controlling dictators, like Joseph Stalin and Mao Zedong. God's leadership style is also different than the type of absolute control a puppet master might have over his puppets. God *controls* people and the course of events, but not in the way one typically imagines. According to the Oxford dictionary, the word *control* can mean "the power to influence or direct people's behavior or the course of events."[10] God leads and controls by inviting, empowering, inspiring, filling, convicting, comforting, challenging, and loving us. God respects our autonomy, our ability to make choices independently, but, at the same time, he persistently and patiently influences us toward his loving will.

Samantha, who had been a Christian for fifteen years, had recently gotten out of her fifth destructive relationship. Her heart was broken, but she refused to go to any type of counseling, she didn't follow the advice of her pastor, and she didn't like "to do that emotional self-reflective stuff." So, after her fifth heartbreak, was she accurate in pointing the blame at God? Would it have been wise to say to her, "God has a reason for it"? I doubt it, although God's reason just might have been because Samantha kept sowing bad seeds and making bad choices. Galatians 6:7 says, "God cannot be mocked. A man reaps what he sows." Samantha made her own decisions and, unfortunately, she might be reaping what she was sowing.

In a mysterious way, however, heartbreak might not be the end of Samantha's story. Proverbs 19:21 says, "Many are the plans in a person's heart, but it is the LORD's purpose that prevails." Perhaps, in spite of all of Samantha's choices, God (who did not cause her situation), in all his loving grace and wisdom, is working through her heartbreak to help her grow, mature, and develop into a beautiful, compassionate, and powerful woman of God. God never gives up on his precious children. God will never give up on you.

God is very much alive and at work in profound and purposeful ways all around us. God does not casually observe our lives from a distance. Rather, he is a deeply present and relational God who is constantly at work in the world, wooing us, calling us, and mending and bending us. As he does so, he heals us and breaks our mental glass ceilings, enabling us to transcend our habitual negative and self-defeating thinking. God is extraordinarily good, magnificently loving, and creatively powerful. His purposes, amidst human choices, will mysteriously and ultimately prevail, eventually leading all creation toward a "new heaven and a new earth" (Rev. 21:1).

My brain cannot even begin to compute how the influence of the enemy, others' and our own choices, and God's will work together. I suppose I am like a caveman trying to comprehend quantum physics. How God's purposes will prevail over our choices and the negative influences of unseen spiritual forces is a mystery that I contemplate in faith.

Speaking of hope, the apostle Paul wrote to the new believers at the church in Thessalonica concerning their relatives who passed away, "Brothers and sisters, we do not want you to be uninformed about those who sleep in death, so that you do not grieve like the rest of mankind, who have no hope" (1 Thess. 4:13). Even though the main thrust of the passage is the resurrection, it also makes an interesting point about grief: the difference between those who do know Christ and those who do not is hope. The rough storms and hurricanes of painful experiences, such as heartbreak and loss, may take their toll, but thank God that is not the last word. Love, whether in this life or the life to come, wins!

The Foundation of Hope

Christian hope, based on the truth of God's Word, should be the foundation and scaffolding for our theology of suffering. The key is to place our hope in truths that God has explicitly stated in the Scriptures and not in wishful thinking (as understandable as those wishes may be). You won't find any verses that say we or our loved ones will never get sick, experience heartbreak, pass away, or be fully content in this life. In fact, Romans 8:22–23 tells us that it is normal to "groan inwardly" because we will never feel fully satisfied living in a sin-sick world. We can, however, have a confident hope in his Word, and that should shape our theology of suffering. Let's explore a few such truths.

A Hope for Blessedness

After a painful breakup, it is easy to feel cursed rather than blessed. We endure sleepless nights obsessing over would-haves, could-haves, and should-haves. We might even feel abandoned by God and think our number has been deleted from his cell phone. The truth, however, is that you might be on his speed dial and uniquely positioned for blessing. In Matthew 5:3–4, Jesus says, "Blessed are the poor in spirit, for theirs is the kingdom of heaven. Blessed are those who mourn, for they will be comforted," and in Matthew 5:6, he says, "Blessed are those who hunger and thirst for righteousness, for they will be filled."

Blessed is an interesting word. Five hundred years before Jesus was born, the Greek poets used it to mean "prosperous, happy, and the state or experience of the gods." Jesus said those who are poor in spirit and those who are experiencing grief, hunger, and thirst can experience blessedness or a godlike state.

You might say to yourself, "Well, I fit the bill—Poor in spirit? Check. Grieving? Check. Hungry and thirsty for God's righteousness in my life? Check, check."

And then you might think, *But I don't feel as if I am prospering or in a godlike state.*

I believe you. But perhaps things are not as they seem.

Poor, hungry, thirsty, and mourning—society doesn't exactly regard these as desirable qualities. Rather, it esteems the wealthy, those who are full of themselves, and those who have it all together. The more wealth you have, the whiter your smile, the greater your physique, the bigger your house, the whiter your picket fence, the broader your investments—these dictate your status in the world. The lie is that the closer you are to those standards of success and perfection, the happier you will be. Jesus, on the other hand, says people who are poor in spirit, grieving, hungry, and thirsty are in the best place to receive blessings. Such people are positioned to be filled with the nearness of God's comforting and reassuring presence in a way others— those who seem to be perfect and have it all together—cannot experience. King David understood this profound truth. He writes, "The LORD is close to the brokenhearted and saves those who are crushed in spirit" (Ps. 34:18).

Although your heartbreak and season of grief might feel like a curse, they are a potential blessing in disguise. If you allow, they could open you up to the opportunity to experience God in a greater measure. While God is present with all people in every moment, he is uniquely present with the heartbroken. God moves close to the suffering, the same way any concerned parent moves close to his or her precious, hurting child.

Your brokenness also allows you to be thirsty, hungry, and open to being filled with God's goodness. Try pouring water into a cup that is already full. It doesn't work. Try offering someone a delicious slice of chocolate cream pie after he or she has just eaten a gourmet meal and a huge banana split. He or she will probably pass. But filling an empty cup and offering food to a hungry and thirsty individual is a different story. In God's economy, less equals the potential for more. Your inner lack is precisely what opens up the possibility for God to fill you with more of himself.

Be encouraged. You are blessed, not cursed. God has not left you high and dry. Rather, he has come low, taken on flesh in the form of Christ, and offered to drench and bless you with the living water of his Spirit. Your unforeseen singleness could be the key that unlocks the door to a profoundly intimate relationship with God. Surrender to the One who can mend your heart and watch him take your intimacy with him to greater depths.

God wants you to experience deeper intimacy with him, but he also wants to fashion something new within and through you.

A Now Hope for a New Kind of You

One day, suffering will cease and we will stand in the presence of an amazing God among a fully restored community of God-lovers for eternity. I can't wait for that day. Fortunately, we can have a taste of it right now. Hebrews 11:1 indicates there is also a *now hope* through a *now faith* for a new kind of you. Your heartbreak might be the end of a chapter, but it is certainly not the end of your story. You can have a hopeful confidence that "he who began a good work in you will carry it on to completion until the day of Christ Jesus" (Phil. 1:6). God is not an absentee landlord or a divine clockmaker who created the world and left it to ticktock without his love and guidance. So take courage. God is holding you, healing you, shaping you, and molding you through your suffering.

God Is Growing You

Covanta is a unique company. Both a waste management and a power company, it turns people's trash into treasure by using it to produce fuel to make electricity in a way that reduces emissions in the environment.[11] The company recently received an award from the Environmental Protection Agency.

Like Covanta, God, mysteriously and wonderfully, produces power from waste. Romans 5:3–5 says, "Not only so, but we also glory in our sufferings, because we know that suffering produces perseverance; perseverance, character; and character, hope. And hope does not put us to shame, because God's love has been poured out into our hearts through the Holy Spirit, who has been given to us." For many, a breakup puts the brakes on what might have been an unhealthy relationship in the first place, allowing a breakthrough to healthier God-inspired possibilities.

Despite your circumstances, or rather because of your circumstances, God is shaping and producing a new kind of you. He doesn't cause evil and give you the garbage of your circumstances, but he can certainly use it to build electric and powerful character. Teresa Pasquale, author of *Sacred Wounds: A Path to Healing from Spiritual Trauma*, writes, "I wish suffering wasn't the doorway to depth and knowing and awakening, but it is the way we were made. It is through the death of something in us that we are reborn. It is through the pain that we have access to something that a superficial life story will never give access to."[12] The painful setback of your heartbreak could actually be a miraculous setup for profound change and the birth of exponential godly growth in your life.

The growth that could happen after your soul experiences trauma is much like the growth that occurs after a hard physical workout. When you push your muscles past what they are accustomed to, they begin to stretch and tear. Assuming you don't overdo your exercise program, your muscles then begin to heal and become stronger than they were before. The same is true for the soul. God created a process in which trauma, loss, and pain can actually build, strengthen, and grow your soul to produce greater character in you. Instead of PTSD becoming a prolonged detriment to your life, God can work through your suffering so you can experience post-traumatic growth. As an old saying goes, "The hotter the fire, the purer the metal." God wants to grow and mature you into someone with deep levels of perseverance, character, and hope—not just for your sake but for the sake of those you encounter on your story-weaving journeys.

To experience this kind of transformation, however, you need to cling to Christ through your suffering and allow him to be the Great Physician and Counselor of your soul. Concerning the healing hope we have in Christ, James White, author of *Grieving: Our Path Back to Peace,* writes, "It is the power that keeps one going, the fuel that runs the engine of the soul, the medicine that brings healing to a wounded heart. It gives strength to face an uncertain future, for it looks not to its own resources, but to Christ."[13] The enemy of your soul comes to steal the joy in your heart, kill the hope in your future, and destroy the liberating work of God in your life. Jesus, on the other hand, came to fill you with immense joy, instill life-giving hope, develop life-giving character within you, give you an abundant life, and increase the kingdom of God.

God Is Growing an Imperfect Kind of You

A new kind of you is not a perfect kind of you, at least as we commonly understand perfection. Sure, we are perfect in Christ, but we will undoubtedly be bumbling and stumbling until we meet him face-to-face (I can imagine myself tripping as I walk through the pearly gates).

Perfection in the biblical sense is more about honesty in our brokenness, in a state of surrender to the grace of God and acceptance of how he sees us, than about a blemish-free life. David Benner writes, "Perfection is not the elimination of imperfection but the ability to recognize, forgive, and include it. Only when we accept the wounds, brokenness, and imperfections can we then discover the wholeness that comes with their inclusion."[14]

When I think about my early college years I remember being an anxious soul, constantly striving for perfection. I was trying to measure up to the status of some ambiguous model of sainthood, desperately seeking the approval of God and those around me. I felt I had to look a certain way, act a certain way, and pray a certain way to be accepted and valued. Rather than focusing on the grace and love of God and my identity in Christ, I had a neurotic and narcissistic type of faith. I was focused mostly on myself, and I was exhausted.

One day a famous visiting author and pastor looked at me with eyes of discernment and compassion. "You will never be perfect, and you will always have issues and junk until the day you die," he said tenderly. "But you are loved." That was profoundly liberating for me to hear, not because it gave me a license to do whatever I wanted whenever I wanted, but because it gave me permission to be real, to be human, and to accept my limitations. It gave me the freedom to accept where I was currently in the sanctification process (being shaped into the image of Christ). His words gave me permission to be honest about my wretchedness, yet still take hold of my blessedness as a God-ordained healing agent on a mission in the world.

No matter how much healing God provides for you, you will probably still have a few cracks in your pot, a bit of fog in the mirror of your soul, and slight defects in your vision. You will always be a wounded healer. And that is okay. The power of the gospel, at least in part, frees you from having to act or strive for perfection. Even the apostle Paul said, "Not that I have already obtained all this, or have already arrived at my goal, but I press on to take hold of that for which Christ Jesus took hold of me" (Phil. 3:12). You don't have to muster up faith, plaster on a perpetual smile, or get it all together. God is not a Hollywood producer demanding perfect scenes and acting prowess. Rather, he desires honest and tender hearts that are bent toward him, and people who are passionately taking hold of all Christ has for them.

As you surrender your heart to God, know that as the Grand Artist he is creatively and gently fashioning a new perfectly imperfect kind of you. Your season of heartbreak can be one of the most transformative experiences of your life. I encourage you to be patient. As a seed takes time to blossom into a beautiful life-giving plant, so God's work in your heart will take time to bring forth something special.

Hope to Be a Blessing

Your heartbreak is not the end of your story. Even though your trial may be very difficult, God wants to instill hope in you that he has destined you to be a blessing to others and to the world. God has a way of using the pain, struggle, and suffering we experience not only for our good but also for the good of others. Similar to Covanta, God uses your garbage for good, causing your negative emissions to decrease and your life-giving energy to increase.

An old saying says, "Hurt people, hurt people. Wounded people, wound people. Free people, free people. And comforted people, comfort people." Whom the world bruises, God comforts, loves, and uses. The apostle Paul knew this truth well. In

2 Corinthians 1:3–4 he encouraged the Corinthians to know God as "the Father of compassion and the God of all comfort, who comforts us in all our troubles, so that we can comfort those in any trouble with the comfort we ourselves receive from God."

God wants you to know that in the midst of your heartbreak and troubles he moves toward you as the Father of compassion, not as the father of lies and condemnation. He wants to comfort you so you can, at some point, comfort and serve others. Just as God chose the wounded nation of Israel to be a blessing to the world, he chose you to be a story-catching ambassador to everyone you come into contact with.

God desires that you be confident and free to shout from the rooftops—whether to your ex, to your circumstances, or to your own inner critic—the truth of Genesis 50:20: "You intended to harm me, but God intended it for good to accomplish what is now being done, the saving of many lives."

You can hope that God will use you to be a blessing. You know what it means to suffer loss and heartbreak, and I pray you will experience what it means to be comforted, to grieve well, and to heal. So many people who are confused and lost in a sea of pain will need the experiential wisdom, character, and hope-filled theology of suffering that you forged in the flames of real living. Don't waste your suffering; give it to God and watch him do extraordinary things with it.

A Future Hope for a New Kind of Love

One day, the fire of God's luminous love will burn away all the seeds of evil that have affected and infected us. Messy relationships, heartbreak, and trauma will be things of the past. Insecurities, doubts, and fears will be no more.

In Revelation 21:4, the apostle John records a profound glimpse of the moment when heaven and earth will be restored, when all will be made whole: "'He will wipe every tear from their eyes. There will be no more death' or mourning or crying or pain, for the old order of things has passed away." There will come a day where God will gently wipe away the troublesome tears from our weary eyes with his strong healing hand. And then there will be no more death, no more loss, no more pain, and no more heartbreak. Wow. That's quite a future to look forward to, isn't it?

What really excites me about that day is that we will finally love one another without our egos, junk, and trauma getting in the way. Faith will replace fear; love will replace hate; purity will replace manipulation; and goodness will replace evil. We will experience the purest intimate relationships with God and others, filled with love, affection, and community. We can hope for, and someday enjoy, a perfect and new kind of love in a place where heartbreak will be a thing of the past.

Epilogue

It is my hope that after reading this book you understand some of the nuances of the grieving process in your season of heartbreak, and that you will prioritize focusing on your love and connection with God, self, and others, and will adopt precious practices that will help you heal and grieve well. I also hope you will become a story catcher and start to wrestle through your own personal theology of suffering when you are ready, not just for your own sake but also for the sake of others.

It takes tremendous courage to grieve well. It is not an easy journey. I remember how much easier it was to run and numb than to deal and feel. I remember how hard it was to face my anger, sadness, and shame. Heck, at times, even joy was scary. I remember being a loner, an island, fearing connection with everyone, even myself. But as I became intentional about my vulnerability and my intimacy with God and others, I found practices that worked for me, and my life started to change. I started to flourish. I started to heal. I started to see myself, God, and others in a different light. The more I reflected and connected with the vertical and horizontal pathways, the more I refracted the love of God and felt a sense of being alive that I wanted to share with others.

Even though I would have told you otherwise, before my healing transformation I wasn't ready for love and marriage. I think it would have been a disaster. I don't think a person is ever truly ready for love and marriage, but I lacked the emotional and spiritual maturity to love someone as she was rather than as my fantasy projection of what I thought she should be. I also had too many unresolved, painful relational traumas that would have gotten in the way of connecting with someone in a loving, living, and life-changing way.

I began receiving profound insights only after I started to take grieving seriously, not just grieving my ex but grieving my other losses as well. And grieving in an intentional and healthy way eventually opened the door for me to receive more of God's lovely surprises.

After coming to a much healthier place in my life, I found and married an amazing, wonderful, and beautiful woman. At the time of this writing, I have been with her for about seven years. I really did find the greater good that God had for me. I am astounded at how God has poured out his grace and given me the desires of my heart for a healthy, holy, and happy marriage. I thank God every day for this relational journey with my wife, and I am amazed that God can create profound triumph from a painful tragedy. He turned an awful mess into an awe-inspiring message.

Some Last Thoughts

You will recover. You will get through the hard times. The fact that you have read this book shows you are hungry for understanding, healing, and growth. That God-given desire to grow and mature will be one of the most powerful resources to get you through the healing process.

If you decide to stay single so you can focus on what God has planned for you, that is awesome. Singleness is not a disease or something you should be ashamed about. You can do many things as a single person that can be difficult to do in a relationship. Date yourself, date God, and have a blast.

If you are anxious about finding love again, take heart. Be patient, grieve well, and move with the leading and rhythm of God's Spirit through your season of heartbreak. Saying "yes" to God in every step of your journey, despite the pain or difficulty, will propel you toward a future of exciting possibilities.

Notes

Introduction

1. Peter Scazzero with Warren Bird, *The Emotionally Healthy Church: A Strategy for Discipleship That Actually Changes Lives* (Grand Rapids: Zondervan, 2003), 50.

CHAPTER 1: Zigzag

1. Bob Sehlinger and Len Testa, *The Unofficial Guide to Walt Disney World, 2015* (Birmingham, AL: Keen Communications, 2015), 103.

2. Brook A. Marcks and Douglas W. Woods, "A Comparison of Thought Suppression to an Acceptance-Based Technique in the Management of Personal Intrusive Thoughts: A Controlled Evaluation," *Behaviour Research and Therapy* 43, no. 4 (2005): 433–45.

3. This is a paraphrase of the well-known "Serenity Prayer," which is most often attributed to German theologian Reinhold Niebuhr.

CHAPTER 2: Ouch! That Hurts!

1. Ethan Kross et al., "Social Rejection Shares Somatosensory Representations with Physical Pain," *Proceedings of the National Academy of Sciences of the United States of America* 108, no. 15 (2011): 6270–75.

2. C. Nathan DeWall et al., "Acetaminophen Reduces Social Pain: Behavioral and Neural Evidence," *Psychological Science* 21, no. 7 (2010): 931–37.

3. Helen E. Fisher et al., "Reward, Addiction, and Emotion Regulation Systems Associated with Rejection in Love," *Journal of Neurophysiology* 104, no. 1 (2010): 51–60.

Notes

CHAPTER 3: Powerful Emotions

1. J. David Creswell et al., "Neural Correlates of Dispositional Mindfulness During Affect Labeling," *Psychosomatic Medicine* 69, no. 6 (2007): 560–65.

2. Matthew Lieberman, "Diaries: A Healthy Choice," *New York Times*, December 12, 2012, http://www.nytimes.com/roomfordebate/2012/11/25/will-diaries-be-published-in-2050/diaries-a-healthy-choice/.

3. Jon Frederickson, *Co-Creating Change: Effective Dynamic Therapy Techniques* (Kansas City: Seven Leaves, 2013), 1.

4. Brian S. Borgman, *Feelings and Faith: Cultivating Godly Emotions in the Christian Life* (Wheaton, IL: Crossway, 2009). Borgman gives a detailed description of the proper place and stewardship of emotions in the Christian life.

5. Brené Brown, *Daring Greatly: How the Courage To Be Vulnerable Transforms the Way We Live, Love, Parent, and Lead* (New York: Gotham Books, 2012), 63.

6. Lewis B. Smedes, *Shame and Grace: Healing the Shame We Don't Deserve* (San Francisco: HarperSanFrancisco, 1993), 1.

7. Ronda L. Dearing and June Price Tangney, eds., *Shame in the Therapy Hour* (Washington, DC: American Psychological Association, 2011), 6.

CHAPTER 4: Shock Absorbers

1. Christopher P. Fagundes, "Implicit Negative Evaluations About Ex-partner Predicts Break-Up Adjustment: The Brighter Side of Dark Cognitions," *Cognition and Emotion* 25, no. 1 (2011): 164–73.

2. Richard Rohr, *The Naked Now: Learning to See as the Mystics See* (New York: Crossroads, 2009), 125.

CHAPTER 5: The Door Is Closing

1. Bruce Ecker and Robin Ticic, *Unlocking the Emotional Brain: Eliminating Symptoms at Their Roots Using Memory Reconsolidation* (New York: Routledge, 2012).

2. The breakup myth became more prominent when Lily gave that same relationship advice to Ted on the show *How I Met Your Mother*, episode 4.9, "The Naked Man."

3. Diana Fosha, "Transformance, Recognition of Self by Self, and Effective Action," in *Existential-Integrative Psychotherapy: Guideposts to the Core of Practice*, ed. Kirk J. Schneider (New York: Routledge, 2008), 290–320.

4. C. S. Lewis, *A Grief Observed* (San Francisco: HarperSanFrancisco, 2001), 69.

CHAPTER 6: The Vertical Pathway

1. Richard Milich and William E. Pelham, "Effects of Sugar Ingestion on the Classroom and Playgroup Behavior of Attention Deficit Disordered Boys," *Journal of Consulting and Clinical Psychology* 54, no. 5 (1986): 714–18.

2. L. Alan Sroufe, "Attachment and Development: A Prospective, Longitudinal Study from Birth to Adulthood," *Attachment and Human Development* 7, no. 4 (2005): 349–67.

3. Todd W. Hall et al., "Attachment to God and Implicit Spirituality: Clarifying Correspondence and Compensation Models," *Journal of Psychology and Theology* 37, no. 4 (2009): 227–42.

4. Reinhard Achenbach, "The Empty Throne and the Empty Sanctuary: From Aniconism to the Invisibility of God in Second Temple Theology," in *Ritual Innovation in the Hebrew Bible and Early Judaism*, ed. Nathan MacDonald (Berlin: De Gruyter, 2016), 52.

5. *Dictionary.com*, s.v. "prodigal," accessed August 6, 2016, http://www.dictionary.com/browse/prodigal.

6. John Dominic Crossan, *The Greatest Prayer: Rediscovering the Revolutionary Message of the Lord's Prayer* (New York: HarperCollins, 2010), 40.

CHAPTER 7: The First Horizontal Pathway

1. Beth Allen Slevcove, *Broken Hallelujahs: Learning to Grieve the Big and Small Losses of Life* (Downers Grove, IL: InterVarsity Press, 2016), 181.

2. Lisa F. Berkman and S. Leonard Syme, "Social Networks, Host Resistance, and Mortality: A Nine-Year Follow-Up Study of Alameda County Residents," *American Journal of Epidemiology* 109, no. 2 (1979): 186–204.

3. Julianne Holt-Lunstad, Timothy B. Smith, and J. Bradley Layton, "Social Relationships and Mortality Risk: A Meta-analytic Review," *PLOS Medicine* 7, no. 7 (2010): e1000316, doi:10.1371/journal.pmed.1000316.

4. James S. House, "Social Isolation Kills, but How and Why?" *Psychosomatic Medicine* 63, no. 2 (2001): 273–74.

5. John T. Cacioppo and William Patrick, *Loneliness: Human Nature and the Need for Social Connection* (New York: Norton, 2008), 92.

6. John Bowlby, *Attachment*, vol. 1 of *Attachment and Loss*, 2nd ed. (London: Hogarth, 1982), 176.

CHAPTER 8: The Second Horizontal Pathway

1. Curt Thompson, *The Soul of Shame: Retelling the Stories We Believe About Ourselves* (Downers Grove, IL: InterVarsity Press, 2015), 13.

2. Jerry Basel and Denise Basel, *The Missing Commandment: Love Yourself* (Grand Rapids: Heart and Life Publishers, 2013), 18.

3. Tania Bright, *Don't Beat Yourself Up: Learning the Wisdom of Kindsight* (Oxford: Monarch Books, 2015), 79.

4. Kim Fredrickson, *Give Yourself a Break: Turning Your Inner Critic into a Compassionate Friend* (Grand Rapids: Revell, 2015), 16.

5. Kristin Neff, *Self-Compassion: Stop Beating Yourself Up and Leave Insecurity Behind* (New York: William Morrow, 2011).

6. Henri J. M. Nouwen with Michael J. Christensen and Rebecca J. Laird, *Spiritual Formation: Following the Movements of the Spirit* (New York: HarperCollins, 2010), 46.

7. Annie Maheux and Matthew Price, "The Indirect Effect of Social Support on Post-trauma Psychopathology via Self-Compassion," *Personality and Individual Differences* 88 (2016):102–7.

CHAPTER 9: Prayer

1. Thomas Merton, *Thomas Merton: Selected Essays*, ed. Patrick F. O'Connell (Maryknoll, NY: Orbis Books, 2014), 238.

2. Thomas Keating, *Open Mind, Open Heart: The Contemplative Dimension of the Gospel* (New York: Amity House, 1986).

3. Thomas Keating, *Centering Prayer: A Training Course for Opening to the Presence of God* (Boulder, CO: Sounds True, 2009), 24.

4. Ibid., 36.

5. Leanne Payne, *The Healing Presence: How God's Grace Can Work in You to Bring Healing in Your Broken Places and the Joy of Living in His Love* (Wheaton, IL: Crossway Books, 1989), 61.

6. Walter Brueggemann, *The Message of the Psalms: A Theological Commentary* (Minneapolis: Augsburg Fortress, 1984), 51.

7. Ibid., 21.

8. Chris Ann Waters, *Seasons of Goodbye: Working Your Way Through Loss* (Notre Dame, IN: Sorin Books, 2000), 116–17.

9. Jaak Panksepp and Lucy Biven, *The Archaeology of Mind: Neuroevolutionary Origins of Human Emotions* (New York: Norton, 2012).

10. John Bowlby, *Attachment*, vol. 1 of *Attachment and Loss*, 2nd ed. (London: Hogarth, 1982), 66.

11. Geoffrey W. Bromiley, *The International Standard Bible Encyclopedia*, vol. 3 (Grand Rapids: Eerdmans, 1988), 64.

12. Kevin F. Brien, *The Ignatian Adventure: Experiencing the Spiritual Exercises of Saint Ignatius in Daily Life* (Chicago: Loyola Press, 2011), 141.

13. Antoine Lutz et al., "Regulation of the Neural Circuitry of Emotion by Compassion Meditation: Effects of Meditative Expertise," *PLOS One* 3, no 3 (2008): e1897, doi:10.1371/journal.pone.0001897.

14. Julieta Galante et al., "Effect of Kindness-Based Meditation on Health and Well-Being: A Systematic Review and Meta-Analysis," *Journal of Consulting and Clinical Psychology* 82, no. 6 (2014): 1101–14.

CHAPTER 10: Holy Huddle

1. W. B. Stiles, "'I Have to Talk to Somebody': A Fever Model of Disclosure," in *Self-Disclosure: Theory, Research, and Therapy*, ed. V. J. Derlega and J. H. Berg (New York: Plenum Press, 1987), 257–82.

2. C. S. Lewis, *A Grief Observed* (San Francisco: HarperSanFrancisco, 2001), 58.

3. Henri J. M. Nouwen, *Out of Solitude: Three Meditations on the Christian Life* (Notre Dame, IN: Ave Maria Press, 2004), 38.

4. Brené Brown, *Daring Greatly: How the Courage To Be Vulnerable Transforms the Way We Live, Love, Parent, and Lead* (New York: Gotham Books, 2012), 113.

CHAPTER 11: Heal: Deal, Feel, Reveal, Seal

1. Melba Colgrove, Harold H. Bloomfield, and Peter McWilliams, *How to Survive the Loss of a Love* (Los Angeles: Prelude Press, 1991), 72.

2. Lysa TerKeurst, *Unglued: Making Wise Choices in the Midst of Raw Emotions* (Grand Rapids: Zondervan, 2012), 44.

CHAPTER 12: Journaling

1. Hannah Stockton, Stephen Joseph, and Nigel Hunt, "Expressive Writing and Posttraumatic Growth: An Internet-Based Study," *Traumatology: An International Journal* 20, no. 2 (2014): 75–83.

2. Stephen J. Lepore and Melanie A. Greenberg, "Mending Broken Hearts: Effects of Expressive Writing on Mood, Cognitive Processing, Social

Adjustment and Health Following a Relationship Breakup," *Psychology and Health* 17, no. 5 (2002): 547–60.

3. Stephen Joseph, *What Doesn't Kill Us: The New Psychology of Posttraumatic Growth* (New York: Basic Books, 2011), 97.

4. Susan Duke, *Grieving Forward: Embracing Life Beyond Loss* (New York: Warner Faith, 2006), 90.

CHAPTER 13: Shut the Front Door

1. Tara C. Marshall, "Facebook Surveillance of Former Romantic Partners: Associations with PostBreakup Recovery and Personal Growth," *Cyberpsychology, Behavior, and Social Networking* 15, no. 10 (2012): 521–26.

2. Ibid., 521.

CHAPTER 14: Forgive to Live

1. Everett L. Worthington, *Forgiving and Reconciling: Bridges to Wholeness and Hope*, rev. ed. (Downers Grove, IL: InterVarsity Press, 2003).

2. Max Lucado, *You'll Get Through This: Hope and Help for Your Turbulent Times* (Nashville: Thomas Nelson, 2013), 117.

3. Xue Zheng et al., "The Unburdening Effects of Forgiveness: Effects on Slant Perception and Jumping Height," *Social Psychological and Personality Science* 6 no. 4 (2015): 431–38.

4. Ross W. May et al., "Effect of Anger and Trait Forgiveness on Cardiovascular Risk in Young Adult Females," *American Journal of Cardiology* 114, no. 1 (2014): 47–52.

5. Erick Messias et al., "Bearing Grudges and Physical Health: Relationship to Smoking, Cardiovascular Health and Ulcers," *Social Psychiatry and Psychiatric Epidemiology* 45, no. 2 (2010): 183–87.

6. Anne Lamott, *Traveling Mercies: Some Thoughts on Faith* (New York: Anchor Books, 1999), 134.

7. Saima Noreen, Raynette N. Bierman, and Malcolm D. MacLeod, "Forgiving You Is Hard, but Forgetting Seems Easy: Can Forgiveness Facilitate Forgetting?" *Psychological Science* 25, no. 7 (2014): 1295–302.

8. C. S. Lewis, *Yours, Jack: Spiritual Direction from C. S. Lewis* (New York: HarperCollins, 2008), 166.

9. James R. White, *Grieving: Our Path Back to Peace* (Minneapolis: Bethany House, 1997), 76.

CHAPTER 15: Serve, Don't Swerve

1. Hao-Jie Song, Jiang-Hong Du, and Yong-Xin Li, "Purpose in Life and Anxiety, Loneliness: Mediator Effect of Boredom," *Chinese Journal of Clinical Psychology* 21, no. 6 (2013): 1033–35. See also Patricia A. Boyle et al., "Purpose in Life Is Associated with Mortality Among Community-Dwelling Older Persons," *Psychosomatic Medicine* 71, no. 5 (2009): 574–79.

CHAPTER 16: In Need of Story Catchers

1. Carl R. Rogers, *A Way of Being* (Boston: Houghton Mifflin, 1980), 142.

2. Abby B. Harvey and Andrew Karpinski, "The Impact of Social Constraints on Adjustment Following a Romantic Breakup." *Personal Relationships* 23, no. 3 (2016): 396–408.

3. Ibid., 404.

4. *IBISWorld*, "Landscaping Services in the US: Market Research Report," February 2016, http://www.ibisworld.com/industry/default.aspx?indid =1497/.

5. Ibid., 8.

6. Shane Hipps, *Flickering Pixels: How Technology Shapes Your Faith* (Grand Rapids: Zondervan, 2009), 114.

7. Jim Plagakis, "A Thoroughly Modern Malady," *Drug Topics* 153, no. 10 (2009): 20.

CHAPTER 17: A Theology of Suffering

1. Marc Klein, *Serendipity*, directed by Peter Chelsom (Santa Monica: Miramax, 2001), DVD.

2. Kimberley Kennedy, *Left at the Altar: My Story of Hope and Healing for Every Woman Who Has Felt the Heartbreak of Rejection* (Nashville: Thomas Nelson, 2009), 30.

3. Max Lucado, *You'll Get Through This: Hope and Help for Your Turbulent Times* (Nashville: Thomas Nelson, 2013), 30.

4. Thomas G. Long, *What Shall We Say? Evil, Suffering, and the Crisis of Faith* (Grand Rapids: Eerdmans, 2014), 133.

5. Walter A. Elwell, *Evangelical Dictionary of Theology*, 2nd ed. (Grand Rapids: Baker, 2001), 1054.

6. Richard Allan Beck, *Reviving Old Scratch: Demons and the Devil for Doubters and the Disenchanted* (Minneapolis: Augsburg Fortress, 2016), 8.

7. Ibid., 8–9.

8. Johannes G. Botterweck, Heinz-Josef Fabry, and Helmer Ringgren, eds., *Theological Dictionary of the Old Testament*, vol. 11, trans. David E. Green (Grand Rapids: Eerdmans, 2001), 279.

9. Gerhard Kittel, Geoffrey W. Bromiley, and Gerhard Friedrich, eds., *Theological Dictionary of the New Testament: Abridged in One Volume* (Grand Rapids: Eerdmans, 1985), 334.

10. Angus Stevenson, ed., *Oxford Dictionary of English*, 3rd ed. (Oxford: Oxford University Press, 2010), 379.

11. Reuben Brewer, "This Power Pioneer Is Turning Trash into Treasure," *The Motley Fool*, April 29, 2014, http://www.fool.com/investing/general/2014/04/29/this-power-pioneer-is-turning-trash-into-treasure.aspx.

12. Teresa B. Pasquale, *Sacred Wounds: A Path to Healing from Spiritual Trauma* (Atlanta: Chalice Press, 2015), 28.

13. James R. White, *Grieving: Our Path Back to Peace* (Minneapolis: Bethany House, 1997), 42.

14. David G. Benner, *Human Being and Becoming: Living the Adventure of Life and Love* (Grand Rapids: Brazos Press, 2016), 10.

About the Author

Mark Gregory Karris is a husband, ordained pastor, licensed marriage and family therapist, writer, recording artist, Red Cross volunteer, worship leader, and all around biophile. A voracious reader and researcher, he received a master's degree in counseling through the Alliance Graduate School of Counseling in Nyack, New York, a master of divinity from Drew Theological School in New Jersey, and is working on his doctor of psychology from Alliant International University in San Diego. Mark currently serves as a therapist, working with individuals, couples, and families in the military; and he travels internationally with the Red Cross, facilitating workshops on stress, trauma, communication, and other relevant topics.